COMPUTER LANGUAGE
REFERENCE GUIDE
Second Edition

Harry L. Helms is the author of seven other books on computers and electronics. He has also written over 100 magazine articles on various topics in electronics for such magazines as *Popular Electronics*, *Elementary Electronics*, and *Popular Mechanics*. A former technical writer for Radio Shack and Texas Instruments, he is currently electronics editor for a major New York publisher. He is a graduate of the University of North Carolina.

COMPUTER LANGUAGE REFERENCE GUIDE

Second Edition

by
Harry L. Helms

Howard W. Sams & Co., Inc.
4300 WEST 62ND ST. INDIANAPOLIS, INDIANA 46268 USA

International Standard Book Number: 0-672-21823-2
Library of Congress Catalog Card Number: 83-51705

Edited by *Welborn Associates*

Printed in the United States of America.

Preface

This edition of *Computer Language Reference Guide* differs in several significant ways from the original. Hopefully, however, it still remains a concise, useful overview of several important programming languages.

Among the new features of this edition are chapters on C and FORTH. The C language has been the subject of widespread interest in recent years while FORTH is becoming increasingly used in such diverse applications as remote control and video games. The chapter on BASIC has been expanded to include extensive coverage of the IBM Personal Computer and Apple II/IIe implementations of BASIC, which have become the de facto standard implementations of the language. Significant revisions and additions have also been made to the chapters on ALGOL, COBOL, FORTRAN, Pascal, and PL/1.

The objective of this book remains the same, however. It is a concise and easily accessible overview of the most significant and widely used programming languages. It presumes you understand at least one of the languages discussed in this book and are familiar with basic computer concepts. If you meet these criteria, this book can serve as your "phrase book" as you "travel" through languages you are not familiar with. It will help you understand what is going on when you are confronted with a program listing written in a language other than the one(s) you normally use. It can also give you a better appreciation and understanding of the strengths and weaknesses of various programming languages.

As in the first edition, one major problem in preparing this book was selecting between the various implementations of computer languages. In this book, an attempt has been made to focus on the most common usages of ALGOL, C, LISP, Pascal, and PL/1. The chapters on COBOL and FORTRAN focus their attention on the latest ANSI standards for each language. The BASIC chapter, by contrast, virtually ignores the ANSI BASIC standard and instead discusses those features of BASIC common to most implementations of the language. Special attention is given to the complete implementations of BASIC for the IBM and Apple IIe microcomputers.

It is common to find that each system will incorporate certain variations in a language, particularly in such areas as number representations, maximum number of significant digits, maximum size of variable names, input/output facilities, and library functions supplied. Thus it is always wise to consult the manual for the system being used for unique features of the language.

Naturally, each language will have its own features that cannot "translate" well into other languages, such as BASIC's interactive capabilities, Pascal's data type flexibility, or FORTRAN's computational abilities with complex numbers. No human language can be translated word-for-word into another language and no computer language can be exactly transformed into a second language. However, it is often possible to compensate for missing features in a language by creative and elegant use of those features which the language does possess.

If you are a BASIC programmer who has been wondering what Pascal is all about . . . or if you are curious about the difference between a PL/1 and COBOL "picture" . . . or if you simply want a quick overview of the broad spectrum of high-level programming languages, then this book is dedicated to you.

HARRY L. HELMS

Contents

CHAPTER 4

CHAPTER 5

CHAPTER 6

CHAPTER 7

CHAPTER 8

CHAPTER 9

APPENDIX

Chapter 1
ALGOL

ALGOL is a contraction of "*algorithmic language.*" It was developed in 1958 by representatives of the Association for Computing Machinery and its counterpart associations in Britain, France, Germany, and the Netherlands. The language they developed became known as ALGOL-68. Further work on the language by American and European groups produced an improved version in 1960 which became known as ALGOL-60. In 1962, several shortcomings and deficiencies were corrected in ALGOL-60; however, the language was still known as ALGOL-60 rather than ALGOL-62. A further revision, with enhanced input/output features, was produced in 1968 and became known as ALGOL-68. However, mainly because of the competition from other languages, the adoption of ALGOL-68 has been very limited. Since most applications of ALGOL have involved the ALGOL-60 implementation, it is the one discussed in this chapter.

In many respects ALGOL is an improvement over other languages such as FORTRAN. Probably the most significant innovation is that of block structure programming. ALGOL programs are blocks of adjoining statements largely independent of each other. Variable names, procedures, executable statements, and declarations apply only to a particular block (and any blocks nested within it). This permits precise definition of the algorithm involved in a program. This feature of ALGOL was a forerunner of the structured programming approach used in teaching many other languages today.

Unfortunately, although there is considerable acceptance in Europe, ALGOL has never achieved widespread use in the United States. Part of the problem is the weakness in handling character data and the relatively primitive input/output procedures. Another problem is that various computer system manufacturers represent ALGOL symbols in different ways, resulting in confusion. Finally, many users and manufacturers have made substantial investments in FORTRAN and are resistant to change.

Today, ALGOL appears to be a dying language. Two languages based upon ALGOL, Ada and Pascal, have substantially the same strengths along with advantages of their own. However, ALGOL still is used to some extent in Europe, and is worth knowing about if for no other reason than its contributions to language development and contemporary programming concepts.

ALGOL Symbols

One problem with ALGOL is that many of the symbols used in the definition of the language are not commonly available on most hardware systems. The definition of the ALGOL language is known as the *reference language*. The way symbols are represented on different hardware systems comprise the *hardware languages*. Finally, when ALGOL programs are published in a journal or book, a *publication language* is used to allow the use of common mathematical tools (such as subscripts) in describing the program.

In this chapter, we will use the reference language symbols. Table 1-1 gives a listing of the reference language symbols and their equivalents in Burroughs and IBM hardware languages.

In the reference language, all ALGOL keywords are lowercase and boldface. In the Burroughs hardware language, lowercase letters are not provided and all keywords, variable names, etc., will be uppercase letters. The IBM hardware language also allows only uppercase letters; in addition, all keywords must be enclosed in single quotes.

Table 1-1. ALGOL Symbols and Burroughs and IBM Equivalents

Reference	Burroughs	IBM
≡	EQV	'EQUIV'
⊃	IMP	'IMPL'
∨	OR	|
∧	AND	&
¬	NOT	¬
:=	:=	:=
⊔	blank space	blank space
+	+	+
−	−	−
×	*	*
/	/	/
÷	DIV	'|'
↑	**	**
<	<	<
≤	≤	<=
=	=	=
≥	≥	>=
>	>	>
≠	NEQ	¬=
⊏	⊏	(/
⊐	⊐	/)

Program Format and Structure

ALGOL was the first well-known block structured language. Blocks may be thought of as independent modules accomplishing specific functions. The form of an ALGOL block is as follows:

```
label begin declaration(s);
    . . .
    statements;
    . . .
    statement
end
```

Label denotes an optional identifying label or name for the program or statement. The block starts with **begin** followed by a declaration defining variables, arrays, and procedures (these will be discussed later). Following the declaration is a semicolon (;). Each following statement also ends with a semicolon except for the last statement in the block. The block terminates with **end**.

Blocks may be "nested" within each other. An example of this is as follows:

```
begin declaration(s);
    . . .
    statements;
    . . .
    begin declaration(s);
    . . .
    statement(s);
    . . .
    end;
    . . .
    statement(s);
    . . .
    statement
end
```

Note when blocks are nested within other blocks the last statement and **end** are followed by a semicolon. Only **end** and the last statement in the "outer" or main block are not followed by semicolons.

The block structure allows for variables to be local to a specific block, or global to the entire program. If a variable is declared within a specific block, the variable can only be referenced by statements in that block; that is, it is local to that block. If a block is nested within another block, a variable may be referenced by all statements in the program provided it is declared following the **begin** statement of the main block and is not declared in any of the blocks nested within the main program block. Such a variable is global to the entire program.

It is possible to use the same variable name in different blocks and have it local to each block by declaring it in each block it is used. However, such usage is poor programming practice since it is easy to confuse which statements reference each declaration of the same variable name.

Nonexecutable comments may be added after any program line ending with a semicolon or after **begin** or **end**. The comment itself follows **comment** and may be any string of symbols as long as the string does not contain a semicolon, **end,** or **else.** However, the comment must end with a semicolon. The word **comment** may be omitted when a comment follows **end.**

Variables, Constants, and Data Types

ALGOL contains the following data types:

integer—a sequence of digits from 0 to 9. It may be preceded with a + or − sign.

real—an integer, decimal, or exponential number, or an integer number plus a decimal or exponential portion.

Boolean—logical values of **true** or **false.**

character—any sequence of ALGOL symbols, not including single quotes, which is enclosed within single quotes.

Variables are values which may change during the program execution while constants do not. These values may be referred to by names consisting of a sequence of letters and/or digits. Each variable name must begin with a letter.

The data type associated with each variable name must be declared through a type declaration. A type declaration consists of the word **real, integer,** or **Boolean** followed by a list of variable names to be associated with that data type. For example, the declaration:

integer abs, val, stat

would establish that abs, val, and stat will contain only integer values.

Arrays

In ALGOL, an array is a group of values referred to by the same variable name. The individual elements of an array are referenced by the variable name followed by one or more subscripts in parentheses. Arrays are established by an **array** declaration:

type **array** variable name range

where type is a type declaration **(integer, real,** or **Boolean),** the variable name is the one selected to identify array elements, and range represents the limits of the array established by the various dimensions in the brackets. If the type declaration is omitted, the array elements are assumed to be real. For example, the declaration:

array SUMS [1:5]

would establish an array with the elements SUMS [1], SUMS [2], SUMS [3], SUMS [4], and SUMS [5]. Additional dimensions can be accommodated within brackets by separating them with commas. The maximum number of dimensions permissible depends upon the computer system being used, not the ALGOL language.

Assignment and Arithmetic Operators

Values may be assigned to variables names by using := . The form is variable name : = expression

where expression is an arithmetic or Boolean expression that returns a single value when evaluated.

Arithmetic expressions use the following arithmetic operators:

+	Addition
−	Subtraction
×	Multiplication
/	Division
÷	Integer division
↑	Exponentiation

Arithmetic operations are performed from left to right in an expression in the following order of precedence:

1. Exponentiation
2. Multiplication and division
3. Addition and subtraction

However, this order of operations may be overruled by the use of parentheses. Operations within parentheses are performed before any others. When parentheses are nested within each other, operations within the innermost set of parentheses are performed first. Operations within the secondmost inner parentheses are performed next, and so forth.

When the / operator is used to perform division, the result is real regardless of the data types of the operands. If the ÷ operator is used, the result is integer and the operands must be integer.

Relational and Logical Operators

Relationships between two arithmetic expressions may be indicated by the following relational operators:

<   is less than
≤   is not greater than
=   is equal to
≠   is not equal to
≥   is not less than
>   is greater than

Logical operators are used to form Boolean expressions having the values of **true** or **false.** Logical operators are used with logical values, Boolean variable types, or arithmetic expressions joined by relational operators. They are as follows:

∧   and
∨   or
≡   is equivalent to
⊃   implies
¬   not

When arithmetic, relational, and logical operators are used together in a series of expressions, operations are performed in the following order:

1. Operations in parentheses
2. ↑
3. ×, /, ÷
4. +, −
5. All relational operators
6. ¬
7. ∧
8. ∨
9. ⊃
10. ≡

Control and Transfer Statements

Normally, ALGOL program execution moves through each line of the program consecutively. However, this may be altered through the use of the various control and transfer statements available in ALGOL.

Control may be unconditionally transferred to another point in the program through the **go to** statement. Its form is

go to label

where "label" is a label for the statement that program control is to be shifted to. A colon (:) separates the label from the statement it identifies.

Control may be transferred depending upon specified conditions through the **if** . . . **then** and **if** . . . **then** . . . **else** statements. The forms are

if Boolean expression **then** statement 1
if Boolean expression **then** statement 1 **else** statement 2

where the Boolean expression evaluates to a **true** or **false** value, statement 1 is any valid ALGOL statement but another conditional statement, and statement 2 is any ALGOL statement.

When the **if** . . . **then** statement is executed, the Boolean expression is evaluated. If the value is **true,** the statement following **then** is executed. If the value is **false,** the statement following **then** is not executed. The **if** . . . **then** . . . **else** statement is similar, but with the provision that if the Boolean expression is **false,** the statement following **else** is executed.

Iteration and Loops

A sequence of statements may be repeatedly performed for a specified number of times. The form for doing this is:

```
for i : = intval step stepval until endval do
    begin
        . . .
        statements
        . . .
end
```

where intval is the initial value of the control variable **i,** stepval is the increment by which **i** increases each time the loop is executed, and endval is the value of **i** which will terminate execution of the loop. If only one statement is to be repeatedly performed, **begin** and **end** may be omitted. Intval may be a negative value.

With the first execution of the loop, the value of stepval is added to intval and becomes the new value of **i.** When the value of **i** exceeds endval, execution of the loop ceases.

It is also possible to have a statement or sequence of statements performed while a Boolean expression returns a value of **true.** The form is:

> **for** variable : = arithmetic expression **while** Boolean
>   expression
>   **do** statement(s)

The arithmetic expression will be performed as long as the Boolean expression has a value of **true.** The statements following **do** are likewise executed while the Boolean expression is **true.**

Functions

ALGOL provides several library functions for various mathematical computations. The following list contains those functions in ALGOL-60; other implementations of ALGOL may provide additional functions.

abs—returns the absolute value of an expression.
arctan—returns the arc tangent of an expression.
cos—returns the cosine of an expression.
entier—returns the entier of an expression.
exp—returns the exponential of an expression.
in—returns the natural logarithm of an expression.
sign—returns the sign (+ or −) of an expression.
sine—returns the sine of an expression.
sqrt—returns the square root of an expression.

Procedures

ALGOL permits users to write and define functions similar to the library functions supplied by ALGOL. These user-defined functions are known as procedures.

Procedures are defined by a procedure declaration. The form is:

type **procedure** name (parameters); value

where type indicates whether the result of the procedure will be **real, integer,** or **Boolean,** name is the name given the procedure, parameters are the parameters used by the procedure, and value designates those parameters (if any) which are assigned to a corresponding actual parameters when the procedure is invoked.

Each procedure is followed by a series of statements, starting with **begin** and concluding with **end.** At least one statement must be an assignment statement assigning a value to the name of the procedure.

Procedures are invoked within an expression by using the name of the function followed by a list of actual parameters enclosed within parentheses. When the procedure is invoked, each occurrence of a parameter in the procedure declaration is replaced by the corresponding actual parameter. The values of the actual parameters are then used in the statements of the procedure.

It is possible to define procedures which invoke themselves in the statements of the procedure. Such procedures are said to be *recursive*.

Input and Output Procedures

In its original form, the ALGOL language included no input and output features; input and output functions were handled through procedures. In 1964, a working group developed a set of standard primitive procedures for the input and output functions that have been widely adopted. Many ALGOL compilers include these procedures; they can be used as if they were statements on most systems.

A common output procedure is **outreal** which is used to output real variables. The general form of this is:

outreal (output device, real variable);

The output device is symbolized by an integer. The real variable is output in floating-point form occupying 15 characters of space, including the positive or negative sign. Similarly, real values can be read into a system with the **inreal** statement, which has the form:

inreal (input device, real variable name);

where the input device is represented by an integer and the real variable will follow all the normal rules for variable names. This procedure will cause input data to be read until a sequence of characters forming a real value is found.

Similar procedures, such as **ininteger, outinteger, outarray,** etc., are available on most ALGOL systems for the input and output of integers and arrays. The procedure named **outstring** allows for the outputting of literals and blank spaces.

Standard Functions

Some ALGOL systems also provide procedures for the following standard functions:

abs—gives the absolute value of an expression.
arctan—gives the arc tangent of a value.
cos—gives the cosine of a value.
exp—gives the exponential function of a value.
ln—gives the natural logarithm of a value.

sign—gives the sign (positive or negative) of a value.
sin—gives the sine of a value.
sqrt—gives the square root of a value.

Reserved Words

General practice calls for avoiding the use of any variable or procedure names that are (or begin with) any declaration, conditional or unconditional expression (or parts of one), standard procedures (such as **abs**), or **begin** and **end**.

Chapter 2
BASIC

BASIC is the most widely used language for microcomputer systems and may be the most widely used programming language in the world. BASIC is an acronym for Beginners All-purpose Symbolic Instruction Code, and was developed at Dartmouth College by Dr. John Kemeny and Dr. Thomas Kurtz as a teaching language. Elements of both FORTRAN and ALGOL were incorporated into BASIC, although it is obvious that BASIC is more like FORTRAN. Like FORTRAN, program control can (and usually does) shift abruptly from one part of the program to the other.

BASIC has powerful interactive features. A BASIC program can "ask" a user for additional data or to select among alternatives. Unlike most other programming languages, BASIC is almost exclusively used on computer systems employing video display terminals (as opposed to punched-card systems commonly associated with such languages as FORTRAN and COBOL).

BASIC also uses many system commands in addition to statements. Statements are the keywords used to compose a BASIC program while commands are keywords affecting the computer system itself. Commands allow the program to be loaded into the computer memory, the cursor to be placed at a desired point on the video terminal screen, and similar functions which do not directly affect the actual program or its execution.

One unfortunate sidelight of the popularity of BASIC has been the development of several different implementations of the language by various microcomputer manufacturers. Many versions of BASIC include graphics statements, sound and music statements, and other features not envisioned by Kemeny and Kurtz. This mutation of BASIC has been perhaps inevitable given the rapid change in microprocessor technologies over the past decade. Still, it remains a fact that one can be a proficient BASIC programmer on one microcomputer system yet unable to program on another without extensive consultation of the second system's documentation.

As such, no attempt will be made to cover all the various implementations of BASIC here. The general features of BASIC common to virtually all systems will be discussed first, and then a look will be given the two most widely used implementations of BASIC—those developed by IBM and Apple Computer for their microcomputers.

Most microcomputer implementations of BASIC include various operating system commands which become de facto extensions of the language and are used similarly to BASIC commands. The documentation for the microcomputer's operating system should be consulted for the precise definitions of operating system commands.

Program Format

Each line in a BASIC program requires a line number, as in the following example:

```
1000 PRINT "EACH LINE MUST BE NUMBERED"
9999 END
```

Line numbers can be any positive number between 0 and 65535 (0 and 32767 on some computers). Good programming practice calls for using line numbers in multiples of ten (10, 20, 30, 40, etc.) so additional statements can be inserted or removed as needed.

Remarks may be inserted into a program with the REM statement. The REM statement is nonexecutable; it has no effect whatsoever on the program. Its sole purpose is to document the program for other users and for future reference. The general form of a REM statement is:

1000 REM THIS IS A PROGRAM TO COMPUTE ACCOUNTS

Program execution starts with a RUN statement. If a line number follows RUN, execution starts at that line number. If no line number is included, program execution starts at the lowest numbered line. Program execution follows the numerical sequence of the statement line numbers until a STOP or END statement is encountered.

Variables may be introduced in a BASIC program as needed. There is no need to declare them before using them. PRINT and OUTPUT statements may likewise be included wherever needed in the program.

Variables and Constants

Constants are generally not recognized as being distinct in the BASIC language. A constant is simply a variable whose value does not change during execution of the program.

Variables are generally significant to only two places in BASIC. Also, all versions of BASIC allow the use of a single letter as a variable. Some versions of BASIC allow a letter and a number to be used as a variable as in Z2, J6, Y9, etc. Other versions allow variables to use up to 255 characters, although only the first two characters may be recognized for distinguishing variables. For example, the variables ALPHA and ALWAYS would be read the same in some versions of BASIC since only the AL would be recognized.

Another variable type is the *string*. Strings are variables that consist of a group of letters or characters. String variable names end with $ to distinguish them from ordinary numeric variables. Some examples are:

AP$ = "JUMP"   ZL$ = "STRING"   VR$ = "VARIABLE"

Some versions of BASIC allow integer variables. These can be used for storing integer values (whole numbers) in the range from −32768 through 32767. Integer variables are indicated by % following the variable, as in Z9%, T4%, E2%, etc.

Another feature of some versions of BASIC is the ability to use *single-precision* (to six significant figures) and *double-precision* (to sixteen significant figures) variables. Single-precision variables are indicated by ! following the variable name (F5!, etc.). Double-precision variables are indicated by # following the variable name, as in D2#, L8#, etc.

Most versions of BASIC allow the assignment of values to variables by simply using the = sign, as in the following examples:

AS$ = "SUM"   P9% = 145   K5! = 0.12345

However, some versions of BASIC require using a LET statement in order to assign values to variables. In this case the previous example must be entered as:

LET AS$ = "SUM"   LET P9% = 145
LET KS! = 0.12345

To help ensure compatibility with other versions of BASIC, good programming practice calls for the use of LET statements.

Values for variables may be numbers of the appropriate type or expressions which evaluate to a numerical value. The exception to this, of course, is string variables.

Operational Symbols

The BASIC language uses the following symbols for arithmetic operations:

+   Addition
−   Subtraction
*   Multiplication
/   Division
↑   Exponentiation

Most versions of BASIC also provide for the following relational operators:

<   Is less than
>   Is greater than
=   Is equal to
<>   Is not equal to
<=   Is less than or equal to
=>   Is greater than or equal to

Also, most BASIC languages allow for Boolean operators, as follows:

AND   Statement is true if both expressions are true.
OR   Statement is true if either expression is true.
NOT   Produces the complement of a statement.

It is also possible to "add" two strings together. This process is known as *concatenation*. Concatenation is accomplished by simply using a +, as in:

```
L$ = "JOIN" + "STRINGS"
```

The most commonly used forms of BASIC also provide for the manipulation of strings through operational symbols:

<   First string precedes alphabetically
>   First string follows alphabetically
=   Equals
<>   Does not equal
<=   Precedes or equals
>=   Follows or equals

Operations in the BASIC language are performed in the following order:

1. Exponentiation.
2. Negation.
3. Multiplication and division in left to right order.
4. Addition and subtraction in left to right order.
5. String operators in left to right order.
6. NOT
7. AND
8. OR

The order of operations may be overturned by using parentheses. Operations in parentheses are performed first, with sets of parentheses in left to right order when nested within each other.

Program Control

Program control statements are used to direct the flow of operations within a program. Many of these set up a repeating loop of some sort. One of the most common types is the FOR . . . NEXT statement. The general form of this loop is:

```
FOR index variable TO final index value
      Body of loop
NEXT
```

This loop will repeat for a fixed number of times beginning with the first value of the index variable and continuing until it reaches the final value of the index variable. The index variable is an integer.

A variation of the FOR . . . NEXT loop is the following:

FOR index variable TO final index variable value STEP value

This variation increases the index variable value in increments that are indicated by the value following STEP. Thus, in

FOR I = 1 TO 1000 STEP 5

the index variable will increase to 1000 in steps of 5 (1, 6, 11, etc.).

A conditional branch statement is IF . . . THEN. It follows the general form:

IF condition THEN consequence

The condition is typically a variable and its relation is to a value or expression (A > 4, B = (C + D), etc.). The condition could be another branching statement, an input or output statement, an expression, STOP or END, etc.

One common consequence of IF . . . THEN is GOTO. GOTO causes an immediate shift of program control to the statement whose number follows GOTO. An interesting variation of GOTO is ON . . . GOTO, which takes the general form:

ON index variable GOTO statement line numbers

An ON . . . GOTO statement causes the program to branch to different lines depending on the value of the index variable. In the following example:

ON I GOTO 10, 20, 30, 40

the program will branch to line number 10 when I = 1. When I = 2, the program will branch to line number 20, and so on.

An ELSE statement is frequently used to shift the program control in the event that a certain condition is not met. In the following example,

```
IF X > 5 THEN GOTO 200 ELSE GOTO 300
```

a value of X equal to 6 would cause a shift to line 200 while a value of X equal to 4 would cause a shift to line 300.

Input and Output Statements

One of the simplest and most versatile output statements is LIST. As the name implies, LIST causes the entire program that is stored in the memory of the computer to be outputted to the output peripheral that is in use. This is a very useful command if you did not write the program being used and you wanted to know what was in the program.

The most commonly used output statement is PRINT. The general form of PRINT is

```
PRINT item list
```

where the item list may consist of variables, numbers, or literals enclosed in double quotes. If variables are in the item list, their numeric values will be outputted, not the letters or characters representing the variable. For example, if X = 50, then PRINT X would produce an output of 50, not X.

The PRINT statement can also be used to cause mathematical operations to be performed. For example, the line

```
PRINT 2 * (10/2)
```

would cause 10 to be outputted.

A variation of the PRINT statement is PRINT @ (pronounced "print at"). This follows the form:

PRINT @ location output list

This causes the output to be printed at a specific location on the video display or line printer. Each individual system will have its own guide to its video display or printer to allow using PRINT @ correctly.

Another variation is PRINT USING. It is used to specify formats of numeric and string values in order to create desired output effects. The general form of this is:

PRINT USING string variable; variable

The string variable in a PRINT USING statement is known as a *field specifier*. It controls the way the variable is printed out. Consider the following set of statements:

```
A1 = 256.76735490
A$ = "###.##"
```

The statement PRINT USING A$; A1 would result in an output of:

256.77

Note that the variable A1 has been printed out to the number of places specified and has been automatically rounded up to the nearest two places. The symbol # is used to specify the position of digits in the field specifier. The decimal point can be placed as needed within the field specifier.

Other symbols used with PRINT USING are:

> Automatically inserts commas every three digits from the right when inserted between the first symbol of field specifier and the decimal point.
>
> ** Will cause all unused spaces to the left of the decimal point to be filled with asterisks when placed before the field specifier.

$$ Will cause $ to be printed before number when placed before the field specifier.

Other symbols preceding the field specifier are allowed in various versions of BASIC.

TAB is used frequently with PRINT. It moves the cursor of the video display or printer horizontally to a desired spot on a line of output.

INPUT is commonly used to enter data into a BASIC language system. The general form of the statement is:

INPUT list of variables

INPUT is used in the following manner:

INPUT A1, B$

The statement requires entering a numeric value followed by a string variable. In a similar manner, variables must be entered in the order that they appear following the INPUT statement. Values entered are assigned to their corresponding variables. An INPUT statement is often used in conjunction with PRINT statements and literals to prompt program users to use entire required data. Attempts to input incorrect data (such as a numeric value into a string variable) will result in an error.

Another data input statement is READ. READ is used in conjunction with a DATA statement to assign values to specified variables. The general form of READ and DATA statements is:

READ variable list separated by commas
DATA data list separated by commas

DATA statements generally follow READ statements but may appear anywhere in the program. Data in a DATA statement must match up with variables in the corresponding READ statement. Otherwise, an error will result.

A RESTORE statement is sometimes used with READ statements. It causes the next READ statement to start over at the first item in the first DATA statement. This allows re-using the same DATA items as many times as needed within a program. The usual form for using RESTORE is:

```
RESTORE
READ variable list
DATA data item list
```

Arrays

An array in BASIC language is defined as a single variable name used to arrange and store several elements of data. The elements may be numbers or strings. Generally, arrays set up a variable name followed by an integer number from 0 through 255. The general form of an array name is NUM(1), NUM(2), NUM(3), etc. These array variables are known as *single-dimension variables*. Array variables such as A (1,2,3) and Z(1,2,3,4) are *multidimensional variables*.

Arrays may be established by using a FOR . . . TO statement in the following manner:

```
FOR index variable TO final index value
LET array variable (index variable) = final index value
NEXT index variable
```

This is a cumbersome method. A much more commonly used method is DIM, a statement that establishes space in memory for an array of the specified number of dimensions and elements. For example, the statement

```
DIM Z(4)
```

would establish the array Z(0), Z(1), Z(2), Z(3), and Z(4). Note that the array will begin at zero, not one.

It is also possible to establish a multidimensional array using

DIM. The statement DIM A(3,4) establishes an array with the following elements:

A(0,0), A(1,0), A(2,0), A(3,0), A(0,1), A(1,1), A(2,1), A(3,1),
A(0,2), A(1,2), A(2,2), A(3,2), A(0,3), A(1,3), A(2,3), A(3,3),
A(0,4), A(1,4), A(2,4), A(3,4)

The DIM statement appears at the beginning of any program using an array. One frequent use of arrays is to store information in a tabular form.

The maximum number of dimensions that an array may take varies among the different versions of BASIC language. However, most versions allow for an array of up to 255 dimensions.

Subroutines

A subroutine is a relatively independent portion of a program. It need only be written in the program once and it can be used as often as necessary. The program "departs" for a subroutine and, then, program control "returns" to the main program when the execution of the subroutine is finished. Subroutines are composed of numbered BASIC statements just like the rest of the program and all of the other rules of BASIC apply.

Subroutines are invoked with the GOSUB statement as follows:

GOSUB line number

This statement causes program execution to branch out to the subroutine. After the subroutine is executed, program control is switched back to the main program by a RETURN statement. Program execution resumes at the next line following the GOSUB. Good programming practice calls for subroutine numbers to be different from those used in the main program. For example, if the main program used three-digit line numbers, the subroutines should use four-digit numbers.

A variation of the GOSUB statement is ON . . . GOSUB. This, like ON . . . GOTO, will shift the program control to different subroutines depending upon the value of an index variable. The general form of this statement is

ON index variable GOTO subroutine line numbers

STOP and END Statements

A STOP statement interrupts the execution of a program and prints the following message on the output device of the system:

BREAK IN line number

A STOP statement is frequently used to stop the execution of a program if an irregular or abnormal condition is encountered, such as a negative score in a series of test results.

An END statement terminates the program execution normally, without any BREAK IN message. Many versions of BASIC require an END as the last statement in a program; good practice calls for it to always be used as the last statement.

Direct Memory Access

Microprocessor-based systems allow the use of POKE and PEEK statements for direct access to memory locations. Memory locations in most systems using BASIC are one byte in size, meaning that they can hold a number from 0 to 255. Most microcomputers have a maximum of 16,000 to 256,000 such locations.

A number of 0 to 255 can be placed in a memory location using a POKE statement. The general form of this is:

POKE memory location, data to be stored

The memory location is a positive integer expression denoting the memory location where the data is to be stored. The data to be stored is a number or expression between 0 and 255.

It is also possible to read the contents of a specific memory location using the PEEK statement. The general form of a PEEK statement is:

variable name = PEEK (memory location to be read)

The effect of a PEEK statement is to read the contents of a specific memory location and assign the value stored there to the variable name.

PEEK and POKE statements have usefulness in controlling external devices and in graphic displays.

Specialized Input and Output Procedures

Some features have been added to the BASIC language as a result of the characteristics of the microcomputer systems that the language is often used on. One characteristic of microcomputer systems is the common practice of connecting peripherals to the central processing unit through various input and output ports. Since many microcomputer systems are based upon 8-bit microprocessors, port addresses fall into the range of 0 to 255. INP and OUT statements allow the program to directly access these ports.

The general form of an INP statement is:

INP (memory address)

which will cause the computer to read the output of the peripheral located at the specified memory address. An INP may be used with other BASIC statements, such as PRINT, to manipulate data outputted by a peripheral.

An OUT statement causes an effect opposite to an INP statement. It sends a bit of data to an output port through an address specified in the OUT statement. The data is then used by a peripheral connected to the output port. The usual form of an OUT statement is:

OUT port address, data outputted

where the port address is an integer between 0 and 255, and the data outputted is a value or expression that can evaluate to an integer between 0 and 255.

Many popular microcomputer systems use tape cassettes for mass storage. This has resulted in the creation of two commands for handling tape cassettes. The first is CLOAD. Its form is:

CLOAD program name

which causes the program following CLOAD to be read from the cassette tape and stored in the random-access memory of the microcomputer. The opposite of CLOAD is CSAVE, which causes a program to be entered onto a tape cassette. Its general form is simply:

CSAVE program name

Machine Language Subroutines

Higher level languages, such as BASIC, have some disadvantages when compared to the lower level (machine) languages that are used by the microprocessor chip itself. Machine language allows certain operations to be done faster than in BASIC and it also allows the performance of some functions that are difficult or impossible to do in BASIC.

BASIC allows subroutines that are written in machine language to be included within the body of a program. These machine language subroutines can be used by either a CALL or

USR statement (which statement is used varies among different versions of BASIC). The general forms are:

CALL (address of machine language subroutine)

or

USR (address of machine language subroutine)

Program control will return to the BASIC program when a RETURN command is reached in the machine language subroutine.

VARPTR is frequently used in conjunction with machine language subroutines. It will give the memory address of a specified variable, allowing it to be readily used by the machine language subroutine. The general form of VARPTR is:

VARPTR (variable name)

Program Editing Commands

The BASIC language includes several features that are designed to simplify program editing and changes when used on systems that use crt terminals for input and output operations. These features vary among different versions of BASIC; only the most common are given here.

An AUTO statement generates line numbers automatically. If no numbers are given after AUTO, line numbering starts at 10 and proceeds in increments of 10. If one number follows AUTO, line numbering starts at that number and proceeds in increments of 10. For example, AUTO 5 would result in line numbers 5, 15, 25, 35, etc., being assigned. It is also possible to specify the number at which the numbering is to start and the increments in which it will be done. For example, AUTO 100, 10 would result in line numbers 100, 110, 120, etc., being assigned.

A CLEAR statement sets the values of all variables, both numeric and string, to zero or "null." It is commonly used during program testing or debugging.

A CONT statement is used to resume the program execution of a program after an END or STOP statement is encountered in a program. On some versions of BASIC, this statement is known as CON.

A DELETE statement is used to remove specific lines from a program. The usual form is:

DELETE beginning line number-ending line number

However, to delete just one line, use:

DELETE line number

There is also a way to delete all line numbers from the first line up to a specific line. Use:

DELETE -line number

The only difference between this and the previous command to delete one line is the addition of a hyphen just before the line number. Thus, one must be careful in using a DELETE statement to avoid accidentally eliminating several lines of the program. On some versions of BASIC, DELETE is called DEL.

An EDIT statement allows changing of a specific line in the program without affecting other lines. The general form is simply:

EDIT line number

A NEW statement removes all program lines from the memory of the computer and clears all variable values. NEW is used simply by entering it into the computer. On some systems, SCRATCH is used instead of NEW.

A RENUM statement allows renumbering of the line

numbers in a program. This is handy when one needs to insert extra statements into a program, yet the existing line-numbering sequence does not leave enough room for the additional lines. The general form of RENUM is:

RENUM first line to be resequenced, first number of new sequence, increment

If the number of the first line to be resequenced is omitted, resequencing will start at 10. The increment is the numerical step by which each line number will increase (25, 50, 75, 100, etc.). On some systems, RENUM is simply REN.

Program Debugging Aids

BASIC language includes aids for tracing program errors and problems. One is DSP, which will cause the value of a variable and the line number where it is executed to be printed out. Its form is:

DSP variable

A TRON statement activates a tracing function that allows the user to follow the flow of program execution. Each time program control shifts to a new line that line number is displayed on the system's output device. This is especially useful when a program contains numerous subroutines and conditional statements, and one needs to confirm that they are actually being executed. TROFF is the command that turns the TRON function off. On some systems, TRON is referred to as TRACE and TROFF is called NOTRACE.

Library Functions

The following is a list of the most common library functions found in the BASIC language. Different versions of BASIC may not incorporate all of these functions or they may have additional functions not listed here.

ABS—result is the absolute value of an expression.

ASC—gives the decimal ASCII value of a string variable.

ATN—gives the arc tangent of an expression.

CHR$—gives a single element string, which has an ASCII value that is given by an expression in the range 0 to 255 (this function is the inverse of ASC).

COS—gives the cosine of an expression in radians.

DEF FN—declares a user-defined function. Both numeric and string variables may be used.

EXP—gives value of natural number *e* raised to a specified power.

INT—gives integer portion of an expression using the largest whole number that is not greater than the expression.

LEFT$—moves characters from the left end of a string into another string.

LEN—gives the length of a string.

MID$—moves characters from the middle of one string into another.

POS—gives the current position of the video terminal's cursor.

RIGHT$—moves characters from the right side of a string into another string.

RND—gives a random number between 0 and 1.

SGN—gives the sign of an expression.

SIN—gives the sine of an expression.

SPACE$—gives a string of spaces, of a length specified by the expression following the function.

SQR—gives the square root of an expression.

STR$—converts a numeric expression to a string.

TAN—gives the tangent of an expression in radians.

VAL—gives the numerical value of a string.

Reserved Word List

Reserved words vary among the different versions of BASIC. As a general rule, any word that is used as a statement, command, function, or debugging aid will be on the reserved word list for that version of BASIC. The following words are on the reserved list for almost all versions:

AND	GOSUB	NOT	RETURN
AUTO	GOTO	ON	RUN
CLEAR	IF	OR	STOP
CONT	INPUT	OUT	TO
DATA	LET	POKE	TAB
DIM	LIST	PRINT	THEN
ELSE	NEW	READ	USR
END	NEXT	REM	WAIT
FOR			

Apple®* Computer Applesoft BASIC

Apple Computer Applesoft BASIC was developed by Apple Computer Corp. for their popular Apple II microcomputer system. It is also used with the Apple IIe microcomputer and by the Franklin line of Apple-compatible microcomputers.

In general, Applesoft BASIC follows the same general rules of BASIC previously discussed. However, Applesoft BASIC includes several graphics and specialized input/output statements.

Applesoft BASIC was written for microcomputers using the 6502 microprocessor as their CPU. Thus, all assembly language routines in Applesoft BASIC should be written in 6502 assembly code.

Commands

Applesoft BASIC includes the following commands:

*Apple is a Registered Trademark of Apple Computer Corp.

CATALOG—Lists directory of files on diskette.

CONT—Causes program execution to resume.

DEL—Deletes program line numbers indicated.

HIMEM—Sets the highest memory address used by BASIC.

LIST—Lists program lines indicated on video display. If no numbers follow **LIST,** entire program is listed.

LOAD—Loads a program from cassette or disk into computer memory.

LOMEM—Sets the lowest memory address used by BASIC.

NEW—Removes current program and all variables from memory.

NOTRACE—Turns off the line tracing editing function.

RUN—Causes program execution to begin. If a line number follows **RUN,** execution begins at that line number.

SAVE—Saves a program from memory onto a cassette or disk.

TRACE—Turns on the line tracing editing function.

Arithmetic Operators

Applesoft BASIC includes the following arithmetic operators:

+   Addition
−   Subtraction
*   Multiplication
/   Division
∧   Exponentiation

Relational Operators

Applesoft BASIC includes the following relational operators:

=	Equals
<	Less than
<=	Less than or equal to
>< or <>	Not equal to
>	Greater than
>=	Greater than or equal to

Logical Operators

Applesoft BASIC includes the following logical operators:

NOT—Makes a true value false and a false value true.

AND—Gives a true value if both expressions are true; otherwise, the value is false.

OR—Gives a true value if either expression is true; gives a false value if both expressions are false.

Statements

Applesoft BASIC includes the following statements:

CALL—Causes execution of an assembly language sub-routine to begin at the address following **CALL.**

CLEAR—Sets all variables to zero or null and resets the stack.

COLOR—Sets screen color as indicated by a following number:

0 = black	8 = brown
1 = magenta	9 = orange
2 = blue (dark)	10 = gray
3 = purple	11 = pink
4 = green (dark)	12 = green
5 = gray	13 = yellow
6 = blue	14 = aqua
7 = blue (light)	15 = white

DATA—Generates a table of data to be input using **READ**.

DEF FN—Allows definition of a user-written function.

DIM—Defines an array.

DRAW . . . AT—Draws a shape "table" at specific location.

END—Ends program execution.

FLASH—Causes video display to alternate between white on black and black on white.

FOR . . . TO . . . STEP . . . NEXT—Defines a loop to be executed.

GETS—Reads input from a single key.

GOSUB . . . RETURN—Calls a subroutine.

GOTO—Causes a branch to line number indicated.

GR—Sets screen to low-resolution graphics mode.

HCOLOR—Sets screen color in high-resolution graphics mode as follows:

0 = black	4 = black
1 = green	5 = varies with monitor
2 = blue	6 = varies with monitor
3 = white	7 = white

HGR—Sets screen to high-resolution graphics mode.

HGR2—Sets screen to high-resolution graphics mode with four lines of text at bottom of screen.

HLIN . . . AT—Draws a horizontal line between points indicated.

HOME—Clears screen and moves cursor to upper left corner.

HPLOT—Plots a dot or line.

HTAB—Moves cursor to left or right to desired column.

IF . . . THEN—Conditionally executes statement following THEN depending upon expression following IF.

IN#—Selects slot for additional input.

INPUT—Reads keyboard for additional input.

INVERSE—Sets video display to black on white.

LET—Assigns value of expression to a variable.

NORMAL—Restores video display to white on black or cancels **FLASH**.

ONERR GOTO—"Traps" a program error by branching to indicated line number when error is detected.

ON . . . GOSUB—Branches to subroutines beginning at line numbers following GOSUB depending on the value of the variable following ON.

ON . . . GOTO—Similar to **ON . . . GOSUB,** but branches to a specific line number rather than subroutine.

PLOT—Draws a dot on the screen in low-resolution graphics mode.

POKE—Writes a byte to memory location specified.

POP—"Pops" a stack.

PR#—Selects slot for additional output.

PRINT—Outputs data to video display.

READ—Accepts data into memory from DATA statements.

REM—Nonexecuted statements to add remarks or comments.

RESTORE—Allows DATA statements to be read again.

RESUME—Continues program execution after an error has been detected with an error-trapping routine.

ROT—Sets the angular rotation of a shape.

SCALE—Sets the scale of a shape.

SPEED—Sets speed of video output to video display.

STOP—Ends program execution.

TEXT—Sets video display to text mode.

VLIN . . . AT—Draws a vertical line.

VTAB—Moves cursor to specified line.

WAIT—Halts program execution until specified bit pattern is received at designated input port.

XDRAW . . . AT—Draws a shape at specified location.

Functions

Applesoft BASIC includes the following functions:

ABS—Returns the absolute value of a number.

ASC—Returns the ASCII code of a character.

ATN—Returns the arc tangent of a value in radians.

CHR$—Returns the character of an ASCII code.

COS—Returns the cosine of a value in radians.

EXP—Returns the value of a number raised to the power of e.

FRE—Returns the amount of free memory.

INT—Returns the integer portion of a real number.

LEFT$—Returns the leftmost characters of a string.

LEN—Returns the length of a string.

LOG—Returns the natural logarithm of a number.

MID$—Returns the indicated segment of a string.

PDL—Returns the value of game paddle input.

PEEK—Reads indicated memory location.

POS—Returns cursor position.

RIGHT$—Returns rightmost characters of a string.

RND—Generates a pseudorandom number.

SCRN—Returns the color code of specified screen location.

SGN—Returns a −1 if an expression is negative, a 0 if it is 0, and a 1 if it is positive.

SIN—Returns the sine of a value in radians.

SQR—Returns the square root of a value.

STR$—Converts a numeric value to a string value.

TAN—Returns the tangent of a value in radians.

USR—Calls an assembly language subroutine.

VAL—Converts a string value to a numeric value.

IBM Personal Computer Advanced BASIC

IBM has developed three versions of BASIC for use with its family of personal computers. Cassette BASIC is an elementary form of BASIC that contains many of the features of BASIC discussed previously in this chapter. Disk BASIC includes several additional features, primarily for making use of disk drive peripherals. Advanced BASIC incorporates all the features of cassette and disk BASIC and adds numerous graphics and sound features. All three versions of BASIC are upwardly compatible; that is, cassette BASIC programs can be executed by systems using disk and advanced BASIC and disk BASIC programs can be executed on machines using advanced BASIC.

Advanced BASIC allows variable names to be significant to forty letters instead of the two in most other BASIC implementations. Thus, variable names can be more literal and less symbolic.

All versions of IBM BASIC are written with the 8088 microprocessor as the CPU. All assembly language routines must be written in 8088 assembly code.

Commands

IBM Advanced PC BASIC includes the following commands:

AUTO—Causes program lines to be automatically numbered.

BLOAD—Loads binary data or machine language data into memory.

BSAVE—Saves binary data or machine language data.

CLEAR—Clears all variables in memory; can also set memory area.

CONT—Causes program execution to resume after a break.

DELETE—Deletes indicated program lines.

EDIT—Allows editing of specified line number.

FILES—Lists directory of files on diskette.

KILL—Deletes specified diskette file.

LIST—Lists lines in a program on video display.

LLIST—Lists lines in a program on printer.

LOAD—Loads specified program into memory.

MERGE—Merged saved program with another in memory.

NAME . . . AS—Renames a diskette file.

NEW—Erases program in memory.

RENUM—Renumbers lines in a program.

RESET—Closes diskette files.
RUN—Causes program to execute.
SAVE—Saves a program on diskette.
SYSTEM—Closes files and returns to disk operating system.
TRON—Turns on line tracing function.
TROFF—Turns off line trace function.

Arithmetic Operators

IBM Advanced BASIC uses the following arithmetic operators:

+	Addition
–	Subtraction
*	Multiplication
/	Floating point division
\	Integer division
^	Exponentiation
MOD	Modulo arithmetic

Relational Operators

IBM Advanced BASIC uses the following relational operators:

=	Equals
<	Less than
=<	Less than or equal to
> < or < >	Is not equal to
>	Greater than
>=	Is greater than or equal to

Logical Operators

IBM Advanced BASIC includes the following logical operators:

NOT—Makes a true value false and a false value true.

AND—Gives a true value if both expressions are true; otherwise, the value is false.

OR—Gives a true value if either expression is true; gives a false value if both expressions are false.

XOR—Gives a false value if both expressions are the same; gives a true value if both expressions differ.

IMP—Gives a false value if the first expression is true and the second expression is false; otherwise, gives a true value.

EQU—Gives a true value if both expressions have the same value; gives a false value if expressions have different values.

Statements

IBM Advanced BASIC includes the following statements:

BEEP—Produces a "beep" sound from the speaker.

CALL—Causes execution of an assembly language subroutine.

CHAIN—Shifts control to another program.

CIRCLE—Draws a circle.

CLOSE—Closes files.

CLS—Clears the screen.

COLOR—Selects video display color in text mode using the following codes:

0 = black	8 = gray
1 = blue	9 = light blue
2 = green	10 = light green
3 = cyan	11 = light cyan
4 = red	12 = light red
5 = magenta	13 = light magenta
6 = brown	14 = light brown
7 = white	15 = bright white

COLOR is also used in the graphics mode to select background and palette colors as follows:

Code	Palette 0	Palette 1
1	Green	Cyan
2	Red	Magenta
3	Brown	White

COM (ON) (OFF) (STOP)—Enables or disables trapping of data received in the communications adapter.

COMMON—Passes variables shared by chained programs.

DATA—Used with READ to input data.

SATE$—Sets date stored in memory.

DEF FN—Defines a user-written function.

DEFDBL—Causes all variables beginning with any letter in a specified range to be treated and stored as double precision variables.

DEFINT—Similar to **DEFDBL**, but causes variables in specified range to be treated as integer.

DEFSNG—Similar to **DEFDBL**, but causes variables in specified range to be treated as single precision.

DEFSTR—Similar to **DEFDBL**, but causes variables in specified range to be treated as string variables.

DEF SEG—Defines a segment of memory.

DEF USR—Defines the starting address of an assembly language subroutine.

DIM—Sets up an array of variables.

DRAW—Draws a figure defined by codes contained in a string.

END—Causes program execution to cease.

ERASE—Eliminates specified arrays.

FIELD . . . AS—Allocates fields in a random buffer.

FOR . . . TO/STEP/NEXT—Defines a loop.

GET—Reads a record from a random file into a random buffer or reads points from an area of the screen of the video display.

GOSUB . . . RETURN—Transfers control to a subroutine.

GOTO—Causes an unconditional transfer to specified line number.

IF . . . THEN/ELSE—Causes conditional execution of

statement following **THEN** (or **ELSE**) depending upon condition following **IF.**

INPUT—Inputs data entered from keyboard.

INPUT#—Reads a data file sequentially and assigns its values to variables in order.

KEY—Assigns a value to a function key.

LET—Assigns a value to a variable.

LINE—Draws a line or box on the video display.

LINE INPUT—Reads a line of keyboard input and assigns it to a string variable.

LOCATE—Positions the cursor.

LPRINT (USING)—Sends output to printer in form specified.

LSET—Moves data from memory to a random file buffer and left justifies any string variable(s).

MID$—Returns a specified number of characters from a string beginning at position indicated.

MOTOR—Controls the motor on cassette storage device.

ON COM . . . GOSUB—Enables an error trapping routine for the communications adapter.

ON ERROR GOTO—Transfers control to line number indicated when an error code is encountered.

ON . . . GOSUB—Transfers control to subroutine beginning at line number indicated when variable following ON is certain value.

ON . . .GOTO—Transfers control to line number indicated in a manner similar to **ON . . . GOSUB.**

ON KEY . . . GOSUB—Enables a trap for a function key.

ON PEN GOSUB—Enables a trap when using the light pen.

ON STRIG . . . GOSUB—Enables a trap for the joystick.

OPEN—Assigns a buffer to a peripheral or file for input and output.

OPEN COM . . . AS—Prepares the communications adapter for use.

OPTION BASE—Sets the lowest subscript limit of an array.

OUT—Sends a byte to a port.

PAINT—"Paints" designated section of the video display a specified color.

PEN (ON) (OFF) (STOP)—Enables or disables the light pen.

PLAY—Plays music of specified note, octave, volume, and duration.

POKE—Sends a byte to indicated memory location.

PRINT—Displays data on video terminal.

PRINT USING—Displays data on video terminal in specified format.

PRESET—Draws a point of desired color on video display.

PSET—Similar to **PRESET**.

PUT—In text mode, writes records to a file; in graphics mode, writes to area of video display.

RANDOMIZE—Seeds the pseudorandom number generator.

READ—Inputs data from **DATA** statements.

REM—Inserts nonexecuted remarks and comments in a program.

RESRORE—Causes a data statement to be re-read.

RESUME—Causes program execution to resume after an error is detected.

RSET—Moves data from memory to a random file buffer and right justifies any string variable(s).

SCREEN—Selects between text, medium, or high-resolution screen on video display.

SOUND—Produces sound of specified length and tone.

STOP—Ends program execution.

STRIG (ON) (OFF)—Enables or disables joysticks.

SWAP—Exchanges values of two variables.

TIME$—Stores current time in memory.

WAIT—Suspends program execution until specified data received at a port.

WIDTH—Sets width of the display on the video terminal.

WRITE—Outputs items in manner similar to **PRINT** but commas are inserted between items.

WRITE#—Outputs data onto a sequential file.

Numeric Functions

IBM Advanced BASIC includes the following numeric functions:

ABS—Returns the absolute value of an expression.
ATN—Returns the arc tangent of a value in radians.
CDBL—Returns a double-precision representation of an expression.
CINT—Returns the largest integer value of an expression.
COS—Returns the cosine of a value.
CSNG—Returns the single-precision representation of an expression.
DEF FN—Allows definition of new functions.
ERL—Returns the line number where an error has occurred.
ERR—Returns an error code when an error occurs.
EXP—Returns the value of the natural number *e* raised to the power specified.
FIX—Returns the truncated representation of an expression.
FRE—Returns the amount of unused memory.
HEX$—Returns the hexadecimal value of an expression.
INT—Returns the integer portion of an expression that is less than or equal to the expression.
LOG—Returns the natural logarithm of an argument.
MKD$—Converts a double-precision number into a string.
MKI$—Converts an integer number into a string.
MKS$—Converts a single-precision number into a string.
OCT$—Returns the octal value of a number.
POS—Returns a number indicating the position of the cursor.
RND—Generates a pseudorandom number.
SGN—Returns a −1 if an expression is negative, a 0 if it is 0, and a 1 if an expression is positive.
SIN—Returns the sign of an expression in radians.

SPC—Returns the number of skips specified.
SQR—Returns the square root of an expression.
TAN—Returns the tangent of an expression.

String Functions

IBM Advanced BASIC includes the following string functions:

ASC—Returns the ASCII code of a character.
CHR$—Returns the character represented by an ASCII code.
CVD—Converts a string to a double-precision number.
CVI—Converts a string to an integer.
CVS—Converts a string to a single-precision number.
FRE—Returns the amount of memory free for string storage when followed by a string variable.
INKEY$—Returns key being depressed on the keyboard.
INSTR—Searches a designated string beginning at point indicated for another designated string and returns position at which string is found.
LEFT$—Returns number of characters specified from a string beginning at the left.
LEN—Returns the length of a specified string.
MID$—Returns specified number of characters from a string beginning at point indicated.
POS—Returns a substring from a string beginning at designated position in string.
RIGHT$**—Similar to **LEFT$, but returns characters beginning from right side of a string.
STR$—Converts a numeric value into a string.
STRING$—Returns a string of specified length and composed of a designated character.
VAL—Converts a string into a number.
VARPTR—Returns the memory address of a variable.

CBASIC

CBASIC is a compiled version of BASIC developed by Compiler Systems, Inc. Since CBASIC is compiled, CBASIC programs execute faster than BASIC (which is interpreted line by line). CBASIC is similar to BASIC in many respects, with the notable exception that line numbers are not required. Line numbers in CBASIC are used in a fashion very similar to their use in FORTRAN.

Chapter 3
C

C is a language developed by Dennis Ritchie of Bell Laboratories. It was originally implemented on a DEC PDP-11 minicomputer using the UNIX* operating system. Today, however, C is implemented on a wide range of computers and operating systems.

C is a relatively small and simple language. For example, C provides no input or output facilities. It also has no facilities to directly manipulate or compare strings, sets, or arrays. Functions must be written to perform such tasks. Fortunately, many systems on which C is implemented have a "library" of functions available to perform various tasks.

C is still in an evolutionary stage of its development. Some features of the language are hardware dependent. In this chapter, we will restrict our discussion to C as it is implemented on DEC PDP-11 systems. One advantage of C is that it is so "efficient" that routines in assembly or machine language are rarely needed. (In fact, C is sometimes referred to as the closest approximation of a portable assembly language now available.) C also tends to be highly portable between various computer systems.

*UNIX is a trademark of Bell Laboratories.

Program Structure

Programs in C are composed of one or more **functions.** The statements that make up a function are enclosed by a pair of braces, { }. The statements that compose a function are separated from each other by semicolons (;). Functions may be nested with other functions so long as the beginning and end of each function is clearly indicated by a pair of braces. However, functions cannot be "defined" inside of other functions (function definition will be discussed later).

Data may be transmitted between functions by *arguments.* Arguments are placed within parentheses following the name of the function. If there are no arguments, an empty pair of parentheses must follow the argument name.

Each program must have a function named **main.** A C program begins execution at **main.**

Comments may be inserted into a program by inserting them between /* and */. Comments do not affect the execution of the program, and are used to clarify the program for those reading the program listing.

The format of a C program is

```
/* this is a comment */
main ( )
    {
        statement;
        statement;
        statement;
        statement;
    }
```

Identifiers

All functions, as well as variables and constants, must be named by an identifier. Identifiers are composed of letters and numerals; the first character of an identifier must be a letter. The underscore character __ counts as a letter. As a general rule, only the first eight characters of an identifier are significant in distinguishing between identifiers (there may be some variations between systems). Capital letters are considered to be different from small letters. No identifier may be a C reserved word.

Variables and Constants

Variables and constants must be named using identifiers. All variables must be declared before they are used in a program; otherwise, an error will result and the program will not execute. A variable declaration has the following form:

```
type variable1, variable2, . . .variableN;
```

where, type indicates the type of each variable and the identifiers for each variable follow, separated from each other by commas. C provides the following types:

int—An integer value. The permitted range of values depends upon the computer system used; a typical range is from -32768 to $+32767$.

float—Values with a decimal or fractional portion. The permissible range of values and number of significant digits depends upon the computer system being used.

double—Values which **float** to double-precision accuracy (usually at least twice the number of significant digits permitted with **float**). The exact number allowed depends upon the computer system being used.

char—Values consisting of a single byte representing one character from the character set of the computer system being used.

There are three *modifiers* which can be used with the four basic data types. They are **short, long,** and **unsigned. Short** and **long** refer to different sizes of **int** values (the exact sizes again depend upon the computer system being used). **Un-**

signed values are always positive and obey the laws of modulo-2 arithmetic. Qualifiers are used in the following way:

```
short int variable identifier;
long int variable identifier;
```

A new name for a type can be used by declaring it with the **typedef** declaration. For example,

```
typedef int BALANCE;
```

would make **BALANCE** a synonym for **int**. **BALANCE** could be used for declarations and other purposes exactly like **int**.

A single variable may hold objects of different types at different times if it is part of a **union**. The form is

```
union optional name {
     type identifier;
     type identifier;
          . . .
     } union identifier;
```

Any of the types specified within the brackets may be assigned to the variable represented by the union identifier. Any of the types assigned to the union identifier may be used in an expression; however, the type used must be the most recent type assigned to the union identifier.

Variables may also be stored as part of a structure (**struct**). A structure is a list of variable declarations enclosed within brackets. A structure definition appears similar to a **union** definition; this is because a **union** definition is really a structure definition. The form of a **struct** definition is

```
struct optional name {
     type identifier;
     type identifier;
          . . .
};
```

Variables declared in the structure are called members of the structure.

Constants are values which do not change during program execution. They can be associated with an identifier by using **#define.** For example,

#define LIMIT 500

would let **LIMIT** represent the constant value of 500. Constants are not defined the same as variables and appear at the beginning of a program before **main.** No semicolon is used at the end of a constant definition.

To help distinguish between constant and variable identifiers, it is normal practice to use lowercase letters for variable identifiers and uppercase letters for constant identifiers.

Constants may be of different data types similar to variables. **int** and **float** have the same definitions for constants as variables. **float** constants may also be written in scientific notation, as in **0.248E3** or **1.741e-9.** Note that the "e" may be an uppercase or lowercase letter.

A **long** constant may be indicated by adding the letter "L" as a suffix, as in **945L.**

C will interpret all floating-point constants to be **double,** and all integer constants too long to be accommodated by **int** will be treated as **long** constants.

Octal and hexadecimal constants may be indicated by prefixes. An **O** prefix indicates an octal value while a prefix of **O** and **x** (**Ox** and **OX**) indicates a hexadecimal value. The **L** suffix can be added to octal and hexadecimal constants.

C also provides for character constants. A character constant is a single character enclosed in single quotes, such as **'a'.** The value of a character constant is equal to the numeric value of the character in the system's character set. A string constant is a series of characters or spaces enclosed in double quotes, as in

"This is a string constant"

Operators

Arithmetic Operators

C provides the following arithmetic operators:

+	Arithmetic
−	Subtraction
*	Multiplication
/	Division
%	Modulus division

Relational, Logical, and Bitwise Operators

C provides the following relational operators:

<	Is less than
<=	Is less than or equal to
>	Is greater than
>=	Is greater than or equal to
==	Is equal to
!=	Is not equal to

If the specified relation is false, the result has the value of 0; if the relation is true, the result has the value of 1.

C also includes operators for handling individual bits as follows:

~	one's complement
|	bitwise inclusive OR
^	bitwise exclusive OR
&	bitwise AND
>>	shift to right
<<	shift to left

These operators may not be used with **double** or **float** variables.

C also includes the **sizeof** operator. It returns the size in bytes of its operand. Its form is

sizeof (value)

When **sizeof** is used with an array, the result is the total number of bytes in the array.

Logical Connectives

C includes the following logical connectives for joining expressions:

&& AND
|| OR

The && connective returns a 1 if both operands are not zero; otherwise, a 0 is returned. The || connective returns a 1 if either operand is not zero; otherwise, a 0 is returned. The result for both is always **int**.

Increment/Decrement Operators

C includes two operational symbols to increase or decrease the value of a variable. The **+ +** symbol increases the value of a variable by 1 while the − − operator decreases the value of a variable by 1. The symbols may be used as prefixes or suffixes. If used as prefixes, they increase or decrease the value of the variable before the variable is used. If the symbols are used as suffixes, they increase the value of the variable after the variable is used.

Assignment Operators

C provides a convenient shorthand for expressing assignment

using **=** and the operators **+**, **−**, *****, **/**, **%**, **<<**, **>>**, **&**, and **|**. For example, the expression

$$x = x + 1$$

may be rewritten as

$$x + = 1$$

Likewise,

$$x = x - 1$$

may be converted to

$$x - = 1$$

The Comma Operator

The comma (,) can also be used as an operator, usually in conjunction with the **for** statement. When used with two expressions, the comma causes them to be evaluated from left to right, and the value and type of the result is the value and type of the right operand. Commas separating variables in declarations, function operators, etc., are not operators.

Pointers and Pointer Operators

Pointers are defined in C as variables containing the address of another variable. C contains two operators used with pointers and addresses.

The first operator, **&**, assigns the address of one variable to another variable. The statement

y = &x;

assigns the address of the variable **x** to the address of variable **y**.

A second operator, *, assigns the contents of one variable to another. A statement such as **x = *y;** will essentially be equivalent to **x = y;.**

Structural Operators

Structures were previously defined. The only operations that can be performed on a structure are taking its address using **&** and accessing members of the structure using two structural operators.

To indicate that a member is part of a structure, the . operator is used. The form is

    structure identifier . member identifier

It is also possible to indicate a pointer to a structure. The form is

    pointer −> member identifier

Conditional Operator

C provides a conditional operator, **?:**, which allows evaluation of expressions in a manner similar to the "if-then-else" construction found in many other languages. The form is

    expression1 ? expression2 : expression3

When executed, expression1 is evaluated first. If its value is true (or nonzero), expression2 is evaluated. The value of expression2 then becomes the value of the entire construction. If the value of expression1 is false (or zero), then expression3 is evaluated and the value of expression3 becomes the value of the entire construction.

Parentheses and Brackets

Operations within parentheses are always performed before other operations. Square brackets [   ] are used to indicate subscripts.

Order of Operations

Operations are performed in the following order of precedence:

1. ( ), [ ], ->, .
2. &, *, −, + +, − −, !, ~, **sizeof**
3. *, %, /
4. +, −
5. >>, <<
6. !=, = =
7. &
8. ∧
9. |
10. &&
11. ||
12. ?:
13. Assignment operators
14. ,

Type Conversion

In C, operands in arithmetic expressions may be of different types. They are converted to a common type according to the following rules:

1. If either operand is **long,** the other is then **long** and the result is **long.**
2. If either operand is **unsigned,** the other is then converted to **unsigned** and the result is **unsigned.**

3. If either operand is **double**, the other is then **double** and the result is **double**.
4. **float** types are converted to **double** (all floating point arithmetic in C is performed as double precision).
5. **short** and **char** types are converted to **int**.
6. All other operands must be **int** and the result **int**.

The goto Statement

C allows an unconditional switch to a labeled statement through the **goto** statement. The form is

```
goto label
    . . .
    . . .
label: statement
```

It is always possible to avoid using **goto** in C, and good programming practice calls for avoiding its use.

Decision-Making Statements

The basic decision-making statement in C is the **if** statement. Its form is

```
if (expression)
    statement;
```

When the **if** statement is executed, the expression in parentheses is evaluated. If the expression is true (has a nonzero value), the statement following **if** is executed.

It is possible to decide between two statements with the **if** . . . **else** construction. Its form is

```
if (expression)
    first statement;
else
    second statement;
```

As with **if**, the expression in parentheses is evaluted. If the expression is true (has a nonzero value), the first statement is executed. If the expression is false (zero), the second statement is executed.

More elaborate decision-making structures are possible with the **else if** construction. The form is

```
if (expression)
     first statement;
else if (expression)
     second statement;
else if (expression)
     third statement;
     . . .
else
     final statement;
```

When this structure is executed, the expressions in parentheses are evaluated in order. When a true expression is evaluated, the statement following it is executed and no further expressions in the structure are evaluated. If none of the expressions are true, the final statement following **else** is executed.

Another way to decide between multiple statements is the **switch** statement. The **switch** statement tests whether an expression matches a specified constant value and transfers control to the statement associated with that expression. Each expression is preceded by **case** and the expression value must be **int.** The form is

```
switch (expression)
     case expression:
          statement;
     case expression:
          statement;
     case expression:
          statement;
          . . .
     default:
          statement;
```

The expression following **switch** is evaluated (its value must be

int). The value is compared to the value of each expression following the **case** prefix. No two **case** prefixes can share the same expression value. If the value following switch and one of the **case** prefixes match, program execution transfers to that **case** prefix. **default** is optional; if included, the statement following **default** is executed if none of the expression values match the expression value following **switch.** It is not necessary that each **case** prefix be followed by a statement. **case** and **default** prefixes can appear in any desired order.

After one **case** prefix is examined, the next **case** is examined. There may be times when it is useful to "leave" the **switch** construction after a certain **case** prefix. This can be done by adding **break** following **case** and any statement following **case**. The form would be

```
case expression:
      statement;
          break;
```

An alternative to the **switch** construction is to use **return.**

Loops

C has several constructs for loops. One is the **do . . . while** construct. Its form is

```
do
      statement
while (expression);
```

When the statement is executed, the expression following **while** is evaluated. If the expression is true, the statement is again executed. If the expression becomes false, the loop terminates.

An alternative form is the **while** construct. Its form is

```
while (expression)
      statement;
```

When executed, the expression following **while** is evaluated. If it is true (nonzero), the statement is executed. The expression is then evaluated once again. When the value of the expression becomes false (zero), execution of the statement ceases. The **while** construct is more commonly used than the **do . . . while** construct.

C also includes a **for** loop construct. The form is

for (first expression; second expression; third expression)
    statement;

The first expression is the beginning value of the incremental loop value. The second expression is evaluated before each execution of the statement. If the value of the expression is zero (false), execution of the loop stops. The third expression specifies a value by which the value of the first expression is incremented each time the loop is executed.

Loops may be "nested" within each other. To exit a loop or nested loops, **break** may be used. With nested loops, **continue** may be used. **continue** causes the next iteration of a **do . . . while, for,** or **while** loop to be executed.

Functions

As stated earlier, a C program is comprised of one or more functions. The functions may communicate by arguments, values returned by the functions, or by external variables. The form of a function is

name (list of variables)
    argument declarations
    {
    declarations and statements
    }

It is possible to have a function without a list of arguments and their declarations and without any declarations and statements.

If a function is called by another function, a value may be returned to the calling function by **return.** Its form is

return (expression)

where expression may be an allowable C expression. However, there is no requirement that the calling function accept the value; it may be disregarded.

C will assume that the value returned by a function is **int.** If another type is desired, it must be declared in the function returning the value and in the calling function. This is done by placing the desired type (**double,** etc.) before the function name. Any variable in the calling function reserving a value from the called function must be of the same type as the called function.

An external variable is one defined outside a function and available to any function in the program. An internal variable is one declared within a function and available for use only within that function. External variables are "permanent"; they return a value from function to function. Internal variables "exist" only when a function is executed and cease to exist when function execution ceases.

External variables provide an alternative way for functions to communicate with each other. An external variable can be defined by defining it in the same file as functions in which it may be used; such external variable definitions must appear before any functions. External variables may appear in a different file than the one where it is used or be referred to before their definition by using the **extern** declaration.

Register and Static Variables

register declarations are a signal to the compiler that a variable will be used frequently. The effect is to place a variable on the processing unit's registers for faster execution. However, the actual use of the **register** declaration depends upon the system hardware; the system documentation must be consulted for precise limitations.

A **static** declaration makes a variable more "permanent" and "private." When used as internal variables, **static** variables stay in existence after a function is executed. Unlike external variables, they cannot be used by other functions. External **static** variables can be used only within the file in which they appear. This makes it possible for other files to use variables with the same identifier without interference.

Reserved Words

auto	extern	sizeof
break	float	static
case	for	struct
char	goto	switch
continue	if	typedef
default	int	union
do	long	unsigned
double	register	while
else	return	
entry	short	

Chapter 4
COBOL

COBOL is an acronym for COmmon Business Oriented Language. It was developed in 1960 under the auspices of the Conference on Data Systems Languages (CODASYL), an effort spearheaded by the Department of Defense to standardize computer languages used by the Department of Defense and its supply contractors. The use of COBOL language was boosted by the Department of Defense when its use was specified in many defense contracts. Since then, its use has spread through business and industry to the point where it may well be the most widely known and used computer language in the world.

The strength of COBOL lies in its abilities when used in file manipulation. Handling large volumes of data (such as financial or inventory records) is a natural for COBOL. COBOL was also designed to make programs as readable as possible for non-programmers; on this point, it may be the best computer language.

The following is excerpted from the 1965 CODASYL COBOL edition published by the U.S. Government Printing Office:

Any organization interested in using the COBOL

specifications as the basis for an instruction manual or for any other purpose is free to do so. However, all such organizations are requested to reproduce this section as part of the introduction to the document. Those using a short passage, as in a book review, are requested to mention "COBOL" in acknowledgment of the source, but need not quote this entire section.

COBOL is an industry language and is not the property of any company or group of companies, or of any organization or group of organizations.

No warranty, expressed or implied, is made by any contributor or by the COBOL Committee as to the accuracy and functioning of the programming system and language. Moreover, no responsibility is assumed by any contributor, or by the committee, in connection herewith.

Procedures have been established for the maintenance of COBOL. Inquiries concerning the procedures for proposing changes should be directed to the Executive Committee of the Conference on Data Systems Languages.

The authors and copyright holders of the copyrighted material used herein

FLOW-MATIC (Trademark of Sperry Rand Corporation). Programming for the UNIVAC® I and II. Data Automation Systems copyrighted 1958, 1959, by Sperry Rand Corporation; IBM Commercial Translator Form No. F28-8013, copyrighted 1959 by IBM; FACT, DSI 27A5260-2760, copyrighted 1960 by Minneapolis-Honeywell.

have specifically authorized the use of this material in whole or in part, in the COBOL specifications. Such authorization extends to the reproduction and use of COBOL specifications in programming manuals or similar publications.

The latest implementation of COBOL is the 1974 ANSI standard, known as COBOL-74. That is the implementation discussed in this chapter. However, the 1968 ANSI standard is still widely used; the systems manual for a particular system should be consulted to determine which implementation is in use.

Program Format

COBOL programs are divided into four divisions: *identification, environment, data,* and *procedure.* Each division may be further split into sections.

The *identification division,* like the name implies, includes material to identify the program. It must include the program name, and it can include any other information such as the author's name, the system written for, the date written, and general remarks or warnings.

The *environment division* lists the input and output files that the program will use and assigns their internal name to an external name using SELECT/ASSIGN TO statements. Additional sections may appear under this division depending upon the computer system being used.

The *data division* gives additional information about the files specified in the environment division. The arrangement of records within files and the arrangement of data within records are described in this division. All variables are also declared here.

The *procedure division* is where the actual computation of the program is performed. All executable statements are found here, and execution proceeds until a STOP RUN statement is found.

Sections may be further subdivided into paragraphs. Each paragraph has a heading name composed of not more than 30 characters. Paragraphs are broken down into sentences of one or more COBOL statements. Each sentence must end with a period followed by a blank space.

Identification Division

The identification division is for identification and documentation purposes only. It does not affect the main body of the program in any way. The minimum identification division is as follows:

```
IDENTIFICATION DIVISION.
PROGRAM-ID.     name.
```

The name may consist of up to thirty characters followed by a period.

While PROGRAM-ID is the only required entry in the identification division, COBOL allows other entries. These follow the same format as PROGRAM-ID, except that the comment following each additional entry may be followed by any combination of characters that end with a period. These additional identification division entries are:

```
INSTALLATION comment
DATE-WRITTEN comment
DATE-COMPILED comment
SECURITY comment
```

Environment Division

The environment division has two sections, the CONFIGURATION SECTION and the INPUT-OUTPUT SECTION.

The CONFIGURATION SECTION specifies the computer used by the program. It differentiates between the computer the program will be executed on (OBJECT-COMPUTER) and the computer on which the program will be compiled (SOURCE-COMPUTER), though in most cases this will be the same computer. The names used to refer to computers are supplied by the computer manufacturer. Additional attributes of the OBJECT-COMPUTER may be defined, including MEMORY SIZE, PROGRAM COLLATING SEQUENCE, and SEGMENT LIMIT.

The environment division allows an optional SPECIAL-NAMES paragraph. This allows defining names for various hardware features. It also permits specifying a currency symbol other than the dollar sign and use of the comma as a decimal point and period in numbers (as is done in certain nations).

The INPUT-OUTPUT SECTION, as its name implies, is concerned with the input and output of data between data files and the computer system. An important paragraph is FILE-CONTROL, which associates files with the peripherals used to read or write to files.

Data Division

The data division contains five sections:

FILE SECTION
WORKING STORAGE SECTION
REPORT SECTION
LINKAGE SECTION
COMMUNICATION SECTION

Of these, the most important entries are FILE SECTION and WORKING-STORAGE SECTION.

The FILE SECTION describes files using file description (FD) entries. These are followed by a structure definition of the records. One mandatory statement following FD is LABEL RECORD. It is used to indicate whether there are any label records in the program. STANDARD means labels for the files exist; OMITTED means no label records exist. In practice, OMITTED is used with card files and print files while STANDARD is used with files on magnetic media.

Thus, normal organization of the FILE SECTION is as follows:

```
DATA DIVISION.
FILE SECTION.
FD file name
      LABEL     RECORD IS        [STANDARD]
                RECORDS ARE      [OMITTED]
   01 record name
      [data descriptions]
```

Each DATA RECORDS clause must be followed by a *level one number* and the record name, as:

```
   DATA RECORDS ARE INVENTORY.
01 INVENTORY.
```

Level one numbers are followed by *higher-level entries* that describe formats for various portions of the record INVENTORY. These descriptions are accomplished through PICTURE statements. Like the name implies, this statement shows the amount of space, the type of characters, and the location of any decimal point.

The following characters are used to compose PICTURE statements:

A: Letter or space.

B: Space.

P: Denotes location of a decimal point outside the data item.

S: Indicates a space for an operational sign. It is always the left-most character and can be used only once.

V: Denotes location of the decimal point.

X: Any character.

9: Number.

Picture characters may be "compressed" by enclosing the number of times a character is repeated in parentheses. For example, 9999V9999 could be written as 9(4)V9(4).

Data pictures are divided into five categories:

1. *Alphabetic*—only contains character A.

2. *Alphanumeric*—only contains characters A, X, or 9. It cannot be all A's or 9's.
3. *Numeric*—only contains S, V, or 9.
4. *Alphanumeric Edited*—only contains A, B, X, or 9.
5. *Numeric Edited*—only contains B, V, 9, *, +, $, comma, or a period.

The PICTURE description of a record follows on the same line as the level number and record name. PICTURE may be abbreviated as PIC. Good programming practice calls for a PICTURE clause to begin in column 40. If a part of a record will never be referred to by name, FILLER may be used in place of a name. FILLER can also be used to define record areas which will contain no data.

It is also possible for a data record to have data arranged in more than one form. Consider the following:

```
    DATA RECORDS ARE INVENTORY.
 01 INVENTORY.
    02 VALUE-LIST.
       03 ITEM-NAME PICTURE A(30).
       03 STOCK-NUMBER PICTURE A(3)9(6).
```

This means that INVENTORY has data stored in a form called VALUE-LIST. Bytes 1 through 30 have only alphabetic characters. This has been assigned the data name ITEM-NAME. The next three bytes have alphabetic characters and are followed by six bytes containing numeric characters. These nine bytes are assigned the data name STOCK-NUMBER.

It is also possible to refer to the same data with different names and pictures by using REDEFINES. In effect, it allows the same storage space to be described by different data descriptions. In the previous example, VALUE-LIST could be redefined as a new name known as ORDER-LIST by the following sentence:

```
 02 ORDER-LIST REDEFINES VALUE-LIST.
```

Higher-level numbers such as 03, 04, etc., follow REDEFINES and contain pictures and other descriptive material.

Level indicators in COBOL are always two digits. For structures following DATA RECORDS ARE statements, level indicators from 01 to 49 are used.

Following the file section is the work-storage section, where structure and variable declarations that are not file records go. Variable names must be declared using a *level 77 description*. These use pictures like file records, as in the following entry:

77 PI PICTURE 9V9(4).

It is also possible to give each variable an initial value by using VALUE:

77 PI PICTURE 9V9(4) VALUE 3.1416.

More complex data structures may be declared in the working-storage section using pictures and level numbers in a manner similar to the data records that we have previously examined. The only restriction here is that more elaborate data structures *must* follow the level 77 descriptions.

The REPORT SECTION is used to specify the physical appearance of a report. A special file definition known as the report definition (RD) is used to specify how the output will appear on the printed page. The LINKAGE SECTION enables two or more COBOL programs to communicate with each other. The COMMUNICATION SECTION allows the acquisition and processing of information through data communications systems. It does this through communications description (CD) entries which specify the source, length, end of message keys, etc., for all information processed through the data communications system. The REPORT SECTION, LINKAGE SECTION, and COMMUNICATION SECTION are all provided for in COBOL by standard modules.

Procedure Division

The procedure division is where the actual computation is done in a COBOL program. The arithmetic operators are similar to those used in other languages:

+   Addition
−   Subtraction
*   Multiplication
/   Division
* *   Exponentiation

COBOL also includes the basic arithmetic statements ADD, SUBTRACT, MULTIPLY, and DIVIDE. These are added to BY, FROM, GIVING, INTO, and TO. Some typical examples are:

```
ADD 3 TO 4 GIVING 7.
MULTIPLY 3.4 BY NUM1 GIVING NEWPRODUCT.
DIVIDE DIV1 INTO DIV2 GIVING DIVANSWER.
```

COMPUTE is often used with the arithmetic operators, as in COMPUTE ITEM1/3. Execution is generally slower when using COMPUTE, however.

ROUNDED, as the term suggests, causes the result of an operation to be rounded to the nearest least-significant digit. ROUNDED must follow the appropriate data name.

COBOL also includes the following relational operators:

>   greater than
<   less than
=   equal to

NOT can be inserted in front of a relational operator to negate the meaning of it.

Program Control Statements

Within the procedure division are found statements that alter the flow of program execution. One such statement is the unconditional GO TO statement, as in the general form:

GO TO data name

However, this unconditional form may be modified by additional statements, such as:

GO TO data name DEPENDING ON data name or statement

It is also possible to modify a GO TO statement when it is executed by an ALTER statement. To use the ALTER statement, the GO TO statement must be the only statement in the paragraph. In the following,

CONTROL-PARAGRAPH.
    GO TO SEQUENCE-1.

the GO TO statement is the only one in CONTROL-PARA-GRAPH. But the statement

ALTER CONTROL-PARAGRAPH TO PROCEED TO
SEQUENCE-2

will cause the GO TO statement to become:

CONTROL-PARAGRAPH.
    GO TO SEQUENCE-2.

Another variation is the GO TO . . . DEPENDING ON . . . statement. Its general form is:

GO TO data names DEPENDING ON data name

For example, the statement

GO TO PARA1 PARA2 PARA3 PARA4 DEPENDING ON VARI-
ABLE

will result in program control shifting to PARA1 if VARIABLE
equals 1, PARA2 if VARIABLE equals 2, PARA3 if VARI-
ABLE equals 3, and PARA4, if VARIABLE equals 4. If VARI-
ABLE does not equal 1, 2, 3, or 4, the GO TO statement is not
executed.

Another common program control statement is PERFORM.
Its general form is simply:

PERFORM paragraph name

which causes the program control to shift to the paragraph
named. A variation of this is:

PERFORM paragraph name THRU paragraph name

which results in the program control shifting to the portion of
the program that is identified. The number of times a PER-
FORM statement is executed can be varied by TIMES, as in:

PERFORM paragraph name, number, or data name TIMES.

A PERFORM statement may also be used in more complex
combinations, such as:

PERFORM para1 THRU para2 VARYING data name FROM
data name BY data name UNTIL condition

where para1 and para2 are paragraph names.

Another variation of PERFORM allows an action to be repeated until a certain condition is met. The form of this is:

PERFORM para1 THRU para2 UNTIL condition

COBOL also allows for conditional shifts of program control.
One common form is:

IF condition THEN statement

A variation of this incorporates ELSE:

IF condition THEN statement ELSE statement

Data can be moved from one area of storage to another by using a MOVE statement. It has the general form:

MOVE data name TO data name

The COPY Statement

The COPY statement allows copying of COBOL text from a "library" of source statements and its incorporation into a COBOL program. The form is:

COPY name [OF or IN] library

In addition, REPLACING may follow the library name to indicate text to be replaced by the new text. BY may follow REPLACING to precisely indicate the new substitution.

COPY can generally appear anywhere in a COBOL program where a sentence or character string may occur, although COPY statements are usually found in the data or procedure divisions.

Subscripts

COBOL allows sets of items within a record to be subscripted. All subscripted items must have the same PICTURE specification. Up to three subscripts may be used, and all subscripts must be positive integer values (although they can be expressed as arithmetic expressions, data names, or numeric literals). Storage for subscripts is set aside by the OCCURS clause. Its form is:

name OCCURS integer TIMES PICTURE definition

Character Strings

The 1974 ANSI COBOL standard includes several new features for handling strings. One is the INSPECT . . . RE-PLACING statement. Its form is:

INSPECT string name REPLACING characters

This statement "inspects" the data item specified and replaces the indicated characters (such as spaces) with other designated characters (such as zeroes). In the 1968 ANSI COBOL implementation, INSPECT was not provided; EXAMINE (deleted in COBOL-74) served a similar purpose.

A variation of INSPECT is the INSPECT . . . TALLYING statement. This statement counts the number of times a character or group of characters is found in a number string.

Strings of characters can be combined using the STRING statement. The form is

STRING name1,name2

where name1 and name2 represent character strings. DE-LIMITED BY can be used with STRING to indicate which part of a set of characters is to be moved.

A string of characters may be subdivided into smaller strings by the UNSTRING statement. The usual form is

UNSTRING name DELIMITED BY string or literal

STRING and UNSTRING statements may also be combined for more elaborate string manipulation and handling.

READ and WRITE Statements

READ and WRITE statements appear in the procedure division. Before they can be used, two files must be allocated for their use by OPEN statements:

```
OPEN INPUT file name
OPEN OUTPUT file name
```

The READ statement moves a data item from a file and makes it available for use by the program. The general form of a READ statement is:

```
READ file name AT END statement
```

The WRITE statement can take several forms, including:

```
WRITE data name
WRITE data name AFTER ADVANCING number LINES
WRITE data name BEFORE ADVANCING number LINES
```

The last two statements control where the data is printed on the output device of the computer system.

Another output statement is DISPLAY. This causes literals to appear in the output to dress up the appearance. For example, the statement DISPLAY "THE ANSWER IS" X. will cause the words THE ANSWER IS followed by the letter X to appear in the output. Some computer systems use single quotes instead of double quotes with the DISPLAY statement.

Reserved Word List

As can be seen, the COBOL language has a very large number of reserved words. This list contains the most commonly used reserved words — other versions of COBOL may have additional or different reserved words. Consult the system manual for the version of COBOL that is in question.

ACCEPT	DATA	IDENTIFICATION
ACCESS	DATE-COMPILED	IF
ACTUAL	DATE-WRITTEN	IN
ADD	DE	INDEX
ADDRESS	DECIMAL-POINT	INDEXED
ADVANCING	DECLARATIVES	INDICATE
AFTER	DEPENDING	INITIATE
ALL	DESCENDING	INPUT
ALPHABETIC	DETAIL	INPUT-OUTPUT
ALTER	DISPLAY	INSPECT
ALTERNATE	DIVIDE	INSTALLATION
AND	DIVISION	INTO
ARE	DOWN	INVALID
AREA	ELSE	IS
AREAS	END	JUST
ASCENDING	ENDING	JUSTIFIED
ASSIGN	ENTER	KEY
AT	ENVIRONMENT	KEYS
AUTHOR	EQUAL	LABEL
BEFORE	ERROR	LAST
BEGINNING	EVERY	LEADING
BLANK	EXAMINE	LEFT
BLOCK	EXIT	LESS
BY	FIRST	LIMIT
CF	FOOTING	LIMITS
CH	FOR	LINE
CHARACTERS	FROM	LINE-COUNTER
CLOCK-UNITS	GENERATE	LINES
CLOSE	FD	LOCK
COBOL	FILE	LOW-VALUE
CODE	FILE-CONTROL	LOW-VALUES
COLUMN	FILE-LIMIT	MEMORY
COMMA	FILE-LIMITS	MODE
COMP	FILLER	MODULES
COMPUTATIONAL	FINAL	MOVE
COMPUTE	GIVING	MULTIPLE
CONFIGURATION	GO	MULTIPLY
CONTAINS	GREATER	NEGATIVE
CONTROL	GROUP	NEXT
CONTROLS	HEADING	NO
COPY	HIGH-VALUE	NOT
CORR	HIGH-VALUES	NOTE
CORRESPONDING	I-O	NUMBER
CURRENCY	I-O-CONTROL	NUMERIC

OBJECT-COMPUTER	RENAMES	STANDARD
OCCURS	REPLACING	STATUS
OF	REPORT	STOP
OFF	REPORTING	SUBTRACT
OMITTED	REPORTS	SUM
ON	RERUN	SYNC
OPEN	RESERVE	SYNCHRONIZED
OPTIONAL	RESET	TALLY
OR	RETURN	TALLYING
OUTPUT	REVERSED	TAPE
PAGE	REWIND	TERMINATE
PAGE-COUNTER	RF	THAN
PERFORM	RH	THROUGH
PF	RIGHT	THRU
PH	ROUNDED	TIMES
PIC	RUN	TO
PICTURE	SAME	TYPE
PLUS	SD	UNIT
POSITION	SEARCH	UNTIL
POSITIVE	SECTION	UP
PROCEDURE	SECURITY	UPON
PROCEED	SEEK	USAGE
PROCESSING	SEGMENT-LIMIT	USE
PROGRAM-ID	SELECT	USING
QUOTE	SENTENCE	VALUE
QUOTES	SEQUENTIAL	VALUES
RANDOM	SET	VARYING
RD	SIGN	WHEN
READ	SIZE	WITH
RECORD	SORT	WORDS
RECORDS	SOURCE	WORKING-STORAGE
REDEFINES	SOURCE-COMPUTER	WRITE
REEL	SPACE	ZERO
RELEASE	SPACES	ZEROES
REMARKS	SPECIAL-NAMES	ZEROS

Chapter 5
FORTH

FORTH was developed by Charles H. Moore in the late 1960s. In 1968, he implemented a version of the language on an IBM computer which only permitted identifiers which were five characters long. Moore considered the language he had developed to be a fourth-generation programming language; however, the restriction imposed by the IBM computer he was using forced him to call the new language FORTH.

FORTH's first major real-world application came when Moore wrote a FORTH program for the National Radio Astronomy Observatory at Kitt Peak, Arizona in 1971. A compiler was soon written to replace the cross-assembler that had been used. In 1973, Moore founded FORTH, Inc., to develop implementations and tools for his language.

FORTH is well-suited for "real world" applications. It is finding wide use in control applications, such as robotics, industrial equipment, monitoring, and remote control. It has also been implemented in various video and computer games. However, its suitability for number processing and computation is poor compared to most other high-level languages. Offsetting this disadvantage to some extent is FORTH's relatively quick execution time and low memory requirements.

One remarkable feature of FORTH is its easy extensibility. New keywords can be defined and added to the FORTH set by the programmer. Keywords supplied with the language can be redefined if desired. New data and operation types can be defined by the programmer.

This flexibility means that it is easy for poor programs to be created in FORTH (although skilled programmers can create very elegant code). FORTH is also a very difficult language to read from a listing; it is also difficult to "translate" properly into other high-level languages due to its many unique features. (Also, some of the standard FORTH keywords may have been redefined by a programmer.) Nevertheless, FORTH is a language of wide potential and utility for many applications that no other high-level language is fully suited for.

Program Structure

The basic unit of FORTH is the word. A word is any group of one or more characters that defines an action or procedure. The action or procedure takes place when the word is executed. Programs are nothing more than one or more consecutive words. FORTH word definitions begin with a colon (:) and end with a semicolon (;). All words and numbers in FORTH must be separated by one or more spaces. FORTH words can be up to 31 characters long and can be composed of letters, numbers, or other characters.

Stacks

Many FORTH operations involve stack manipulation. A stack is an area of computer memory where numbers are stored in a manner similar to a stack of plates. The first number entered into a stack goes to the "bottom" of the stack (much like the first plate in a stack of plates becomes the bottom of the stack of plates). Additional numbers are placed "on top" of numbers previously placed on the stack. The last number entered into the stack (the one "on top of" the stack) would be the first number removed from the stack (just as the last plate added to a stack—the plate on top of the stack—would be the first plate removed when the plates were finally unstacked). This type of stack is known as a "LIFO" (last in, first out) stack.

Reverse Polish Notation

FORTH makes use of reverse polish notation, the same type of mathematical notation found on many Hewlett-Packard calculators. RPN, as it is commonly called, requires all operators to follow operands. For example, the common addition operation of

$$3 + 2$$

would be written in RPN as

$$3\ 2\ +$$

The results for both would be identical, however, namely 5.

A number in FORTH is an integer value between -32768 and $+32767$. FORTH also provides for double numbers, which contain a decimal point.

Arithmetic Operations

FORTH includes the following operators to be used with RPN to perform arithmetic operations:

+	Addition
−	Subtraction

*	Multiplication
/	Division
**	Exponentiation
MOD	Modulo Division
U/MOD	Unsigned Division
*/	Multiply, then Divide (Integer Result)
*/MOD	Multiply, then Divide (Give Remainder)
NEGATE	Reverses sign of a number
DNEGATE	Same as NEGATE, both work on double numbers
ABS	Gives absolute value of a number
MAX	Selects the largest of two or more numbers
MIN	Selects the smallest of two or more numbers

Stack Manipulation Words

FORTH includes several words for manipulating numbers in the stack. They are as follows:

DEPTH: Counts numbers on the stack.

DROP: Deletes top number on stack. (2DROP is used for double numbers.)

DUP: Duplicates the top number on the stack. (2DUP is used for double numbers.)

OVER: Copies second number to top of the stack. (2OVER is used for double numbers.)

PICK: Copies the designated number to the top of the stack.

ROLL: Rotates the designated number to the top of the stack.

ROT: Rotates third number to the top of the stack. (2ROT is used for double numbers.)

SP @ : Leaves the address of the top of the stack.

SWAP: Swaps the two top numbers of the stack. (2SWAP is used with double numbers.)

SO: Leaves the address of the bottom of the stack.

Constants and Variables

To establish a constant in FORTH, the form is:

n CONSTANT name

where n is a number and the name is a series of up to 31 characters.

A variable is named in the following manner:

VARIABLE name

where name again is any sequence of up to 31 characters. To give an initial value to a variable, the following form is used:

n variable name !

where n is the initial value of the variable and ! is an operator causing a number to be stored in memory at an indicated address.

Arrays are set up in FORTH by allocating additional bytes of memory for them. This is done by following the variable definition with ALLOT, as in the following manner:

VARIABLE name
number of bytes ALLOT

Memory Operations

FORTH includes several operators and words which operate directly on the system's memory. The operators include:

@	Fetches number stored at designated address
!	Stores number at designated address
?	Displays number at designated address

+!   Adds specified value to number at address given
C@   Fetches byte at indicated address
C!   Stores least-significant byte at indicated address
2@   Fetches double number at specified address
2!   Stores double number at specified address

FORTH also includes the following memory operation words:

BLANKS: Fills number of consecutive bytes indicated with blanks.
CMOVE: Copies number of bytes indicated starting at first memory location to a second memory location.
DUMP: Displays contents of indicated memory locations.
ERASE: Fills designated number of consecutive bytes with zeroes.
FILL: Fills designated number of consecutive memory bytes with designated byte.
MOVE: Similar to CMOVE, but operates on numbers instead of bytes.

Control and Transfer Words

FORTH conditional statements depend upon a flag value located at the top of the stack. FORTH defines a value of 1 to be a true flag while a value of 0 is a false flag.

A common conditional construct is BEGIN. . .UNTIL. It has the form

    BEGIN. . .[flag] UNTIL

This causes the operation contained between BEGIN and UNTIL to be repeated until the flag becomes true.

A similar construction is BEGIN. . .WHILE. . .REPEAT. Its form is

    BEGIN. . .[flag] WHILE. . .REPEAT

This causes the action between BEGIN and REPEAT to be repeated until the flag becomes false.

FORTH also includes a variation of the IF. . .THEN construct found in many other languages. The form is

   [flag] IF. . .THEN

where the words between IF and THEN are executed if the flag is true. A variation on this construct is

   [flag] IF. . .ELSE. . .THEN

where words between IF and ELSE will be executed if the flag is true; if the flag is false, the words between ELSE and THEN will be executed.

FORTH also allows a variation of the "DO loop" structure found in many languages (such as FORTRAN, PL/1, and Pascal). The general form is

   [endval] [startval] DO. . .LOOP

In the above, startval represents the beginning value of the loop counter and endval represents the final desired value of the loop counter plus one. When executed, each time the words between DO and LOOP are executed, one is added to startval. When endval is reached, loop execution stops.

FORTH allows the counter value to be copied onto the stack as desired. To do so, I is added to the words between DO and LOOP.

Normally, the DO. . .LOOP construct is incremented by +1. This can be changed in the following manner:

   [endval] [startval] DO. . . .n + LOOP

where startval is the beginning value for the loop counter (that is, the first number on the stack), endval is the final value of the loop counter, and n is the value by which the counter is changed each time +LOOP is executed. If n is negative, the endval could be less than startval.

Defining New FORTH Words

As mentioned before, FORTH allows new words to be defined and for existing FORTH words to be redefined. The form for doing this is

: definition name   word(s) ;

The definition name can be up to 31 characters long without blanks. This is followed by a list of already defined FORTH words that define the action performed by the newly defined word. Note that each definition begins with a colon (:) and ends with a semicolon (;). Comments may be added to a definition by placing them in parentheses; these have no effect upon the execution of words within the definition.

All newly defined FORTH words are compiled and become part of the FORTH word "dictionary" of each compiler. Thus, the words are available to use in future FORTH programs for the compiler without having to define them again. Unneeded FORTH words may be deleted from the compiler by preceding the name of the word by the FORTH word FORGET.

Input and Output Words

The basic FORTH output word is EMIT. It has the form

character EMIT

and will cause the character to be sent to the output device currently being used.

The basic input word is KEY. This accepts a character of input (usually from a keyboard) and places that character on top of the stack. Its form is

    KEY character

A more elaborate output word is TYPE. It has the form

    address n TYPE

where address is the starting memory address and n is the number of characters to be transmitted to the current output device.

A more elaborate input word is EXPECT. This alerts the system that a stream of characters will be on the way. The form is

    address n EXPECT

where address is the starting memory address where the characters are to be stored and n is the number of characters to be stored. A "return" signal can also stop storage of characters in memory.

FORTH also includes additional features which allow specification and formatting of output.

Chapter 6
FORTRAN

FORTRAN is an acronym for FORmula TRANslator. It is one of the oldest high-level languages and is still one of the most widely used.

The first implementation of FORTRAN, FORTRAN I, was developed in 1954 and was first used in 1956 on an IBM 704 computer. In 1958 an enhanced version known as FORTRAN II was introduced. FORTRAN II was followed a few years later by FORTRAN III. However, FORTRAN III was never put into any widespread use.

A major advance was the development of FORTRAN IV in 1962. Thanks to its implementation on IBM systems, it soon achieved wide use. Also in 1962, the American Standards Association organized a committee to develop a uniform version of FORTRAN. In 1966 the committee completed its work, and the result became known as ANSI FORTRAN or FORTRAN-66.

Following 1966 there were several teaching versions of FORTRAN developed. Particularly noteworthy were WATFOR and WATFIV, designed at the University of Waterloo (Ontario). Several other variations of FORTRAN were also developed. These culminated in a revision of FORTRAN in

1977 which became known as FORTRAN-77. It replaced FORTRAN-66 as the ANSI version of FORTRAN. FORTRAN-77 incorporates several of the most useful features of WATFOR and WATFIV.

Early versions of FORTRAN were quite limited in their ability to edit output data into the desired forms, although later revisions have improved capabilities in this respect. FORTRAN also is more limited in its ability to process alphabetic data. Finally, FORTRAN programs often have several abrupt shifts in program control from one area of the program to another, increasing the likelihood of errors and often making a FORTRAN program difficult for others to understand. Balanced against these shortcomings are the still-impressive mathematical computation abilities of the language.

Program Format

Line numbers are frequently used in the FORTRAN language, although there is no requirement that each line be numbered. Line numbers as large as 99999 may be used. Unlike some other languages, there is no "begin" keyword to denote the start of a FORTRAN program. Each program must be terminated with END, however.

There is no requirement in FORTRAN for all variables to be declared in a single section or for all input/output statements to be grouped together. Variables may be introduced in the program as required and values can be assigned to them within the program or through data input into the program. Output can be made where desired. Subprograms that are completely independent programs in their own right must be placed after the main program, and before any data.

There is no punctuation placed at the end of a FORTRAN line. Commas can be used to separate items (variables, numbers, etc.) on the same line. Since FORTRAN was developed for use on keypunch systems, FORTRAN statements follow rules based on 80-character keypunch cards. Statements are written in spaces 7 through 72 of a program line. If a statement must be longer than this, it may be continued on the next line by inserting a character, other than zero, in the sixth space from the left side of the line on which the statement is continued. Good programming practice calls for using $ in the sixth space for statement continuations. Spaces 73 through 80 of each program line are unused.

Statement labels are placed in the first five spaces from the left of each line. Nonexecuted comments can be placed in a program by placing a C in the first space at the left of each line. Spacing between items in a statement is not important since the FORTRAN language ignores blank spaces.

Variables

The two most commonly used variable types in the FORTRAN language are integer and real. Variable names must begin with a letter and can be a combination of up to six letters or numbers; some versions of FORTRAN allow longer variable names to be used but only the first six characters are recognized for differentiating between variable names.

An integer variable can be established simply by beginning the variable name with the letters I, J, K, L, M, or N. Thus, MM, INT, INT22, and LENGTH are all integer variables. They can contain only integer values. Real variables can be established by beginning the variable name with a letter *other than* I, J, K, L, M, or N. Thus, TOTAL, SUM5, and P1981 are all real variables. Real variables can contain integer values as long as they are in real form; i.e., 12.0 instead of 12.

It is possible to "override" the foregoing restrictions outlined above by a *type declaration statement*. For example, DELTA would normally be the name of a real variable. However, it may be declared an integer by using the following statement:

INTEGER DELTA

In a similar fashion, a variable name that would ordinarily be an integer can be declared to be real.

Type declaration statements can be used to establish the following types of variables as well:

Double-Precision—a real value with sixteen significant digits instead of seven. It is written in exponential form using the letter D instead of E.

Complex—a value comprised of a real number component and an imaginary number component. A complex value is represented by two real values.

For example, the expression

$$(1.7, 7.98)$$

represents the complex value

$$1.7 + 7.98i$$

Logical—a constant or variable that can assume one of two values, .TRUE. or .FALSE.

Character—a value that is a string of characters enclosed in single quotes, as in

'CHARACTER'

If a single quote is desired within a string, two consecutive single quotes should be used to indicate it. Thus, the string VARIABLE'S NAME could be represented as 'VARIABLE''S NAME'.

Some systems also provide for variables whose values are octal and hexadecimal numbers.

The type of a variable must be declared before its use in the program or in a subprogram. This does not apply, of course, if one lets the system automatically assign variable types (I through N for integer, remainder of the alphabet for real).

Values for variables may be assigned simply by use of the = symbol:

```
INTSUM = 45
TOTAL = 423.557
```

Values for variables may be assigned as the result of computation or because of input into the computer by READ and DATA statements (to be discussed later).

A constant is simply a variable whose value does not change. Constants follow the same general rules as variables.

Type Declarations

As mentioned before, FORTRAN has the intrinsic ability to specify whether a constant or variable name is integer or real by the first letter of the name. However, there may be situations where one wishes to have an integer variable name beginning with A or a real constant name such as IXT. Also, the programmer needs a way to specify names which represent complex constants, logical variables, etc. FORTRAN handles such situations through the TYPE and IMPLICIT declarations.

The TYPE declaration specifies the data type to be represented by a variable name. The form is

```
type variable name(s)
```

where type is INTEGER, REAL, CHARACTER, DOUBLE PRECISION, COMPLEX, or LOGICAL. Suppose one wished to declare the variable name VECTOR as a complex type. The form would be

```
COMPLEX VECTOR
```

In a similar situation, suppose one wished to declare TEST1 and TEST2 as logical constants. The form would be

```
LOGICAL TEST1, TEST2
```

The IMPLICIT declaration allows the specification of all variable and constant names beginning with a given first letter as being of a certain type. The form is

IMPLICIT type (letters)

where type is REAL, COMPLEX, etc., and the letters are the first letters of the variable names to be of the type specified. The letters in parentheses may be separated by commas (A, B, D, F) or by a dash if a range of letters is to be declared. For example, (A, B, C, D, E, F) is equivalent to (A–F).

It is possible to overturn the effect of an IMPLICIT declaration for specific constant or variable names by a following TYPE declaration. For example, the program lines

IMPLICIT DOUBLE PRECISION (A–Z)
COMPLEX VECTOR, FUNC

would declare all constant and variable names to be double-precision, with the exception of FUNC and VECTOR, which are declared to be complex.

Arrays

An array in FORTRAN is a group of data referred to by a single variable name. Individual items of the group are referred to by the variable name followed by one or more numbers in parentheses. The numbers in parentheses are known as subscripts. An array may have up to seven subscripts. Each subscript is separated from the other by commas.

Arrays are established by the DIMENSION statement. The general form is

DIMENSION variable name (first subscript, second subscript, etc.)

For example, the statement DIMENSION ABLE (2, 3) would

establish an array with the elements ABLE (1, 1), ABLE (1, 2), ABLE (1, 3), ABLE (2, 1), ABLE (2, 2), and ABLE (2, 3).

All subscripts must be integers, integer expressions, or integer nonsubscripted variables.

DIMENSION statements must appear at the beginning of a program, before all executable statements.

It is also possible to express the subscripts of a DIMENSION statement in terms of lower and upper boundaries. For example, the statement

```
DIMENSION YEAR (1952 : 1982)
```

would set up an array having the elements YEAR (1952), YEAR (1953), YEAR (1954), etc., up through YEAR (1982).

Assignment of Values

Often it is necessary to assign an initial value to a variable name. This can be done by the DATA statement. It has two forms:

```
DATA variable names/values
DATA variable names/values, variable names/values, etc.
```

If several variable names are to be assigned the same value, the repeater symbol may be used to save space. The repeater symbol is an integer specifying the number of repetitions plus an asterisk before the value to be repeated. For example, the statement

```
DATA A, B, C, D, E /5 * 1.5/
```

would assign the value of 1.5 to the variable names A, B, C, D, and E.

Variable names must agree with the type of data being assigned to them by a DATA statement. For example, if a real value is assigned to a variable name beginning with I, an error will result.

DATA statements must be placed after specification statements such as DIMENSION but before any executable statements.

Operational Symbols

The FORTRAN language uses the following symbols for arithmetic operations:

+	Addition
−	Subtraction
*	Multiplication
/	Division
* *	Exponentiation

Operations are performed from left to right in the following
order:

1. Exponentiation.
2. Multiplication and division.
3. Addition and subtraction.

The order may be altered by the use of parentheses. Operations
in parentheses are performed first.

FORTRAN allows arithmetic operations involving both
integer and real values. (This is known as mixed-mode arithmetic.) However, the result will be a real value.

If a fractional part is obtained from integer division, it is truncated. For example, 5/2 will give a result of 2, not 2.5.

The = symbol can be used in arithmetic expressions to indicate the outcome of an operation and to assign the outcome to a
variable name. For example, the expression 5/2 = A would result in the value of 2.5 being assigned to A. Initial values may be
assigned to variables by using = instead of a DATA statement,
as in A = 2.5.

FORTRAN also includes several logical operators (sometimes

referred to as relational operators). These are used to compare two expressions and give a result of true or false. Logical operators are:

.LT.	Less than
.LE.	Less than or equal to
.EQ.	Is equal to
.NE.	Not equal to
.GE.	Greater than or equal to
.GT.	Greater than
.NOT.	Negates
.AND.	Both
.OR.	Either

Unconditional Control Statements

Statements in a FORTRAN program are normally executed in the order in which they appear in a program. However, it is possible to interrupt the normal sequence by the use of control statements. Unconditional control statements alter the sequence of execution regardless of other factors in the program.

The most commonly used unconditional control statement is STOP. STOP causes execution of the program to terminate. A STOP statement is not the same as END; END is a nonexecutable statement that merely marks the end of the program for the compiler.

Another common unconditional control statement is GO TO (sometimes written GOTO). The GO TO statement has three variations: unconditional, conditional, and assigned.

Unconditional GO TO Statement

The unconditional GO TO statement causes program control to shift to the statement whose line number follows GO TO. The statement

GO TO 100

will cause the program to immediately shift to line number 100 and execute the statement. The program would next execute the statement immediately following the one on line number 100 and continue executing succeeding statements in a normal manner.

Conditional GO TO Statement

The unconditional GO TO is executed when found in a program regardless of other conditions. In contrast, the conditional GO TO shifts program control to various line numbers depending upon the value of an index variable. Its form is

GO TO (line numbers), index variable

where the line numbers within parentheses are separated from each other by commas and the index variable is an integer variable.

In a conditional GO TO statement, program control shifts to the first line number within parentheses if the value of the index variable is 1. If the value of the index variable is 2, program control shifts to the second line number in the parentheses. If the index variable value is 3, control shifts to the third line number, and so forth. If the value of the index variable is greater than the number of line numbers in parentheses, the next statement immediately following the conditional GO TO is executed. The following is an example of a conditional GO TO statement.

```
GO TO    (50, 20, 75) N
          ↑   ↑   ↑  ↑
IF  N =   1   2   3  4
                      The statement immediately
                      following is executed
```

Assigned GO TO Statement

The assigned GO TO statement requires the use of two statements: GO TO and ASSIGN. The general form of an assigned GO TO statement is

ASSIGN first variable TO second variable GO TO second variable (line numbers)

where the first and second variables are both integer variables. The first variable can be an integer constant as well. The ASSIGN statement must be executed before the assigned GO TO statement is executed.

The ASSIGN statement transfers the value of the first variable to the second variable, which is then used in the assigned GO TO statement. The assigned GO TO statement then shifts program control to one of the line numbers within parentheses depending upon the value of the second variable in a similar fashion to the computed GO TO statement. However, the value of the second variable must be one of the line numbers within parentheses. Further, the name for the second variable must not be used for another purpose within the program.

Conditional Control Statements

The most common conditional control statement is IF. The general form for it is:

IF condition   consequence

A statement such as IF NSUM .EQ. 50 GO TO 99 would cause the program control to shift to statement number 99 whenever the variable NSUM equaled 50.

One variation of the general IF statement is known as the *arithmetic IF*. This will cause program control to shift depending upon the outcome of a mathematical operation. Its general form is:

IF mathematical operation   statement 1, statement 2, statement 3

When an arithmetic IF is executed, the mathematical operation is performed and a value is obtained. If the result is negative, program control shifts to statement 1. If the value is zero, program control shifts to statement 2. If the value is positive, program control shifts to statement 3. Statement numbers must be separated by commas.

Another variation is the *logical IF*. There are two general forms of logical IF statements. The first is:

IF relational expression   consequence

An example of this is

IF (NSUM**2.LT.SUM*NSUM) PRD/A

The relational operation will be performed and a result (true or false) obtained. If the result is true, the operation following the relational operation is also performed. If the value is false, the second operation is not performed.

A second form of logical IF has the format:

IF relational expression   statement 1, statement 2

The relational expression gives a value of true or false when evaluated. If it is true, program control shifts to statement 1. If it is false, control shifts to statement 2. (This second form of the logical IF statement is not available on all FORTRAN systems.)

DO Loops

Another common conditional control construction is the *DO loop*. DO loops utilize a DO statement of the form:

DO statement label   index variable
first value, last value, increment

DO loops are terminated by a CONTINUE statement. Thus, a typical DO loop may look like this:

```
     DO 25     I = 1, 100, 2
     PRINT, NSUM
25   CONTINUE
```

The DO loop just discussed will cause the variable NSUM to be output on the printer or video terminal of the system. The loop will begin with the index variable at 1 and will continue until the index variable reaches a value of 100. The index variable will increase in increments of 2 each time the loop is performed, meaning that the loop will be performed a total of 50 times before the index variable reaches 100.

Any number of statements can be inserted between DO and CONTINUE. If the index variable is to increase in steps of 1, there is no need to include the increment. Thus, DO 50 K = 1, 25 will cause the loop to be executed in steps of 1 for a total of 25 times.

Extended Control Statements

Some versions of FORTRAN provide for additional conditional control statements involving DO loops. One is the IF/THEN/ELSE statement. It has the general form:

```
IF condition THEN DO
statements
ELSE DO
statements
END IF
```

In this case, the condition is evaluated by the computer. If the condition is met, the statements following THEN DO are executed. If the condition is not met, the statements following ELSE DO are executed. The END IF statement serves a function similar to CONTINUE in an ordinary DO loop, serving simply to terminate the loop.

The WHILE/DO statement allows for the executing of a loop as long as a specified condition is met. It has the general form:

```
WHILE condition DO
statements
END WHILE
```

with END WHILE serving to terminate the loop.

The DO CASE statement may be thought of as a multiple DO loop. It has the general form:

```
DO CASE index variable
first group of statements
CASE
second group of statements
CASE
third group of statements
. . .
END CASE
```

The index variable can assume integer values such as 1, 2, 3, etc. If the value is 1, the first group of statements will be executed. If the value is 2, the second group of statements will be executed, and so forth, for all values that the index variable takes. If the index variable takes a value not covered by a CASE statement, then none of the statements in the DO CASE loop are executed. If desired, a group of statements may be included under an IF NONE DO statement that is placed after the last CASE statement and its group of statements. The statements following IF NONE DO will be executed if the index variable falls outside the range of values provided for in the DO CASE loop.

A convenient feature of some versions of FORTRAN is PAUSE. This statement temporarily stops execution of a program and causes the word PAUSE to be displayed on the output device of the computer system. The form of this statement is

```
PAUSE integer constant
```

where the integer constant has five or fewer digits. PAUSE is used to allow the computer operator to change storage tapes or disks, check on program results at a desired point, etc.

Subprograms

FORTRAN allows routines to be written separately from the main program and for these routines to be used by the main program. This allows a desired function to be obtained as needed without writing the same group of statements each time.

FORTRAN allows two types of subprograms: functions and subroutines. Functions return only one result while subroutines can return more than one result.

Functions

Functions are created using the FUNCTION statement. The form is

```
FUNCTION name (dummy arguments)
      . . .
Valid FORTRAN statements (except FUNCTION, SUB-
      ROUTINE, and BLOCK DATA statements)
      . . .
RETURN
      . . .
END
```

in which name follows the same rules as those for constant and variable names. The dummy arguments are variable names used within the function to represent values "transferred" to the function from the main program. The type of result (real, complex, etc.) must agree with the name following FUNCTION. If not, the appropriate type declaration (REAL, COMPLEX, etc.) must precede FUNCTION. Also, there must be one statement within the function that assigns the function name to a value.

In the main program, the function is referred to by its name. Suppose we have defined a function named RATIO as follows:

```
FUNCTION RATIO (A, B)
RATIO = A/B
RETURN
END
```

Suppose in the main program we wish to use the function RATIO with the values 15 and 2 and assign the result to the variable name RESULT. The statement to do so would be

```
RESULT = RATIO (15, 2)
```

In the function RATIO, A would have a value of 15 and B would have a value of 2. After the function is executed, the name RATIO would have a value of 7.5 in the main program. The value of RATIO would then be assigned to RESULT.

Subroutines

Subroutines are similar to functions, but can return more than one result. The most common form of a subroutine is:

```
SUBROUTINE name (subroutine variables)
statements
RETURN
END
```

Any name that is a correct variable name can be used to name a subprogram. A RETURN sends the program control back to the point where the subroutine was "called" by the main program. An END marks the end of the subroutine, the same way it does in the main program.

The subroutine variables are "dummy" variable names used within the subroutine itself. The values of the subroutine variables are "transferred" to variables in the main program whenever the subroutine is used. Subroutines are used by employing the CALL statement. The general form of the CALL statement is:

```
CALL subroutine name (arguments)
```

The arguments in parentheses in the CALL statement may be variables or actual numbers. If the argument is a variable, the value of the variable is transferred to the subroutine variable. If the argument is a number, the subroutine value assumes the value of that number.

Suppose that a subroutine has been written to find the factorial of a number. It can be declared, along with a subroutine variable X, in the following manner:

```
SUBROUTINE FACTOR(X)
statements
RETURN
END
```

This gives the name FACTOR to the subroutine. In the main program, the factorial of 10 can be found by writing:

```
CALL FACTOR(10)
```

which causes the value of 10 to be transferred to X. Once the factorial of X is found, the value is "transferred" back to the main program.

As mentioned earlier, arguments can be variables as well. For example, suppose the variable INTSUM had the value 10. Thus, the statement, CALL FACTOR(INTSUM) would have the same result as CALL FACTOR(10). In the former case, the value of INTSUM would be transferred to X within the subroutine and then "transferred back" once again to the main program after the subroutine had been performed. The result of using CALL FACTOR(INTSUM) and CALL FACTOR(10) would be the same — the factorial of 10.

It is possible to have main programs and subprograms share the same storage locations for data through the COMMON statement. The form is

```
COMMON names
```

where names represent the list of data to be shared by both the main program and subprogram(s). Suppose the statement

    COMMON X, Y, Z

appears in the main program. To refer to the same data storage locations in a subprogram, the statement

    COMMON X, Y, Z

or

    COMMON A, B, C

may be used, although normal practice is to use the same variable names for both main program and subroutine COMMON statement. Corresponding variable names must agree in type.

It is also possible to reserve "blocks" of COMMON storage by labeling such blocks. The form is

    COMMON/label/names/label/names

where both the labels and names follow the rules for naming constant and variable names. The label COMMON is useful when subprograms need to share only a portion of the data common to the main program and subprograms. In such a case, the subprogram COMMON statement will have the label(s) of only the data storage locations common to that subprogram and the main program.

Data may be entered into a labeled COMMON statement through a BLOCK DATA subprogram. The form is

    BLOCK DATA
        . . .
    DATA, DIMENSION, IMPLICIT, TYPE, SAVE, EQUIVALENT,
    COMMON, PARAMETER statements
        . . .
    END

The BLOCK DATA statement will define initial values for the main program and subprograms.

The EQUIVALENCE statement can also be used to indicate that two variable names share the same memory location. The statement

EQUIVALENCE (A, B, C)

would reserve the same memory locations for the variable names A, B, and C.

Variables in a subprogram that are not in an unlabeled COMMON statement or in the argument list are "lost" when control returns to the main program. These can be retained by the SAVE statement. Its form is

SAVE subprogram name

or

SAVE variable name(s)

If the subprogram name follows SAVE, all variables in the subroutine are saved. Otherwise, only the variable(s) specified will be retained.

FORTRAN contains many "built-in" functions, which are known as intrinsic functions. These will be discussed later. However, there may be occasions when it is necessary to use the name of an intrinsic function, a user-defined function, or subroutine in the argument list of a subprogram call. Since subprogram names and variable names follow the same rules, the compiler cannot distinguish between the two unless an INTRINSIC or EXTERNAL statement is used. The form for both is either INTRINSIC or EXTERNAL followed by the name to be declared. INTRINSIC is used with the FORTRAN-supplied intrinsic while EXTERNAL is used with user-defined subprograms.

It is possible to enter a subprogram through a point other

than the normal entry point using the ENTRY statement. The ENTRY statement is placed within the subroutine at the desired alternate entry point(s). The form is

    ENTRY name (dummy arguments)

and it may be accessed by a CALL statement in the same manner as an ordinary subroutine.

Remote Block Units

Remote block units are like subroutines, except that they are not separate programs in their own right, and they do not "communicate" with the main program through arguments. A remote block unit follows the form:

    REMOTE BLOCK name
    statements
    END BLOCK

where the name can be any valid variable name. A remote block can be established anywhere in the main program. It can be used simply by placing the name of the remote block after an EXECUTE statement.

Library Functions

FORTRAN language includes several library functions. Many of these functions are to be used only with certain types of expressions, such as real, complex, etc. The usual form of a function is

    function (expression)

The following is a listing of functions by type:

Complex Functions

CABS—Returns the absolute value of an expression.
CCOS—Returns the cosine of an angle in radians.
CEXP—Exponential (e) raised to power of the expression.
CLOG—Returns the natural logarithm e of the expression.
CMPLX—Converts expression to complex number.
CONJ—Returns the conjugate of a complex function.
CSQRT—Returns the square root of the expression.
CSIN—Returns the sine of an angle in radians.

Integer Functions

IABS—Returns the absolute value of an expression.
IDIM—Returns the positive difference between two values.
IDINT—Converts a double-precision value to integer.
IFIX—Converts a real value to integer.
INT—Truncates the decimal part of a value.
ISIGN—Transfers the sign from one integer value to another.
MAX0—Selects the largest of several values.
MIN0—Selects the smallest of several values.
MIN1—Selects the smallest of several values but converts
    any real result to integer.

Double-Precision Functions

DABS—Returns the absolute value of an expression.
DACOS—Returns the arc cosine of an expression.
DASIN—Returns the arc sine of an expression.
DATAN—Returns the arc tangent of one argument.
DATAN2—Returns the arc tangent of two arguments.
DBLE—Converts an expression to double precision.
DCOS—Returns the cosine of an argument in radians.
DCOSH—Returns the hyperbolic cosine of an argument.
DDIM—Returns the positive difference between two argu-
    ments.

DEXP—Returns the exponential (e) raised to the power of the expression.

DINT—Truncates the decimal part of an expression.

DLOG—Returns the natural logarithm e of an expression.

DLOG10—Returns the common logarithm of an expression.

DMAX1—Selects the largest of several values.

DMIN1—Selects the smallest of several values.

DMOD—Returns the remainder from division by two values.

DNINT—Returns the whole number closest in value to the expression.

DPROD—Converts a real value to double-precision.

DSIGN—Transfers the sign from one value to another.

DSIN—Returns the sine of an expression in radians.

DSINH—Returns the hyperbolic sine of an argument.

DSQRT—Returns the square root of an expression.

DTAN—Returns the tangent of an argument in radians.

DTANH—Returns the hyperbolic tangent of an expression.

IDINT—Converts the expression to the nearest integer value.

Real Functions

ABS—Returns the absolute value of an expression.

ACOS—Returns the arc cosine of an expression.

AIMAG—Returns the imaginary part of a complex number.

AINT—Truncates the decimal part of an expression.

ALOG—Returns the natural logarithm of an expression.

ALOG10—Returns the common logarithm of an expression.

AMAX1—Selects the largest value of several arguments.

AMIN1—Selects the smallest value of several arguments.

AMOD—Returns the remainder from division of two values.

ANINT—Returns the nearest whole number in value to the argument.

ASIN—Returns the arc sine of an argument.

ATAN—Returns the arc tangent of an expression in radians.

ATAN2—Returns the arc tangent of two arguments in radians.

COS—Returns the cosine of an argument in radians.

COSH—Returns the hyperbolic cosine of an argument.

DIM—Returns the positive difference between two arguments.

EXP—Returns the exponential (e) raised to the power of the expression.

FLOAT—Converts an expression to a real number.

NINT—Returns the nearest integer value.

REAL—Converts a complex value to a real value.

SIGN—Transfers the sign from one value to another.

SIN—Returns the sine of an argument in radians.

SINH—Returns the hyperbolic sine of an argument.

SQRT—Returns the square root of an argument.

SNGL—Converts a double-precision value to a single-precision value.

TAN—Returns the tangent of an argument in radians.

TANH—Returns the hyperbolic tangent of an argument.

Character Manipulation

Earlier, the data type CHARACTER was defined as a value that is a string of characters enclosed in single quotes. Difficulties in handling character data had long been a weakness of FORTRAN; however, FORTRAN-77 includes several new features for manipulating character (or string) data.

Two character strings may be concatenated by the concatenation operator //. Suppose that

$$A = 'ABC' \quad B = 'CBA'$$

thus

$$C = A//B$$

would result in

$$C = 'ABCCBA'$$

It is also possible to obtain a substring of a character string. The form is

substring name = string name (int1 : int2)

where substring name is the name to identify the substring, string name identifies the string the substring is to be taken from, int1 identifies the position of the beginning of the substring, and int2 identifies the position of the end of the substring. Suppose there is a character string DIGITS = '1 2 3 4 5 6 7 8'. Thus

INTS = DIGITS (2 : 7)

would produce the substring INTS = '2 3 4 5 6 7'.

There are four intrinsic functions for comparing two character strings. Their form is

function (string1, string2)

and each function returns a value of .TRUE. if the condition described is met. They are as follows:

LGE—The first string is equal to the second string or follows it in collating sequence.

LGT—The first string follows the second in collating sequence.

LLE—The first string is equal to the second or precedes it in collating sequence.

LLT—The first string precedes the second in the collating sequence.

There are also four intrinsic functions for manipulating character data, as follows:

CHAR—Converts a single digit to a character.

ICAR—Converts a single character to a string.

INDEX—Returns an integer indicating the starting position of a substring in a longer string. The form is

INDEX (string, substring)

where string and substring are represented by variable names.

LEN—Returns the length of a character string.

Input and Output Statements

The basic output statement in the FORTRAN language is WRITE. The general form of a WRITE statement is:

WRITE (output medium, statement label) variable(s)

The parentheses include two numbers. The first number specifies the medium to be used for the output. For example, 1 could be a video terminal; 2, a printer; 3, a disk storage device; etc. The second number is a statement label.

Another common output statement available on many FORTRAN systems (although not all) is PRINT. Its form is simply:

PRINT, first variable, second variable, etc.

A PRINT statement also allows the outputting of character data simply by enclosing it in single quotes. The statement

PRINT 'CHARACTER OUTPUT'

would result in CHARACTER OUTPUT appearing on the output device.

The basic input statement is READ. Its form on most systems is simply:

READ, first variable, second variable, etc.

Each READ statement starts reading a new line of input and continues reading until a value has been assigned to each variable following READ.

Values may also be assigned to variables by the DATA statement. The DATA statement is not executed when the program is run; it merely sets up a memory location for each variable name and value when the program is compiled. The general form of a DATA statement is:

DATA variable names /values/

For example, the statement DATA A, B /2.4, 3.78/ assigns A a value of 2.4, and B the value of 3.78.

Formatted Input and Output

Input and output in FORTRAN language is usually "formatted." This means that it is possible to specify exactly how the computer will read input data and the form in which data will be output. This is done with the FORMAT statement and *field descriptors*. The general form of the FORMAT statement is:

label FORMAT (field descriptors)

FORMAT statements always follow input and output statements. A typical form of a statement might be as follows:

WRITE (50) NSUM
FORMAT (I4)

When executed, the WRITE statement will cause the variable NSUM to be output in the form specified by statement 50. Statement 50 has a field descriptor of I4. This means that four spaces are to be used to output NSUM in an integer form. If NSUM has a value of 1234, all four spaces will be used. If

NSUM has a value of 99, only two of the four spaces will be used. The output in such case will be *right-justified*, meaning that 99 will appear in the two spaces furthest to the right. The two "leftover" spaces to the left will be blank.

Sometimes a field descriptor may not be adequate for the desired output. Suppose, in the above example, that NSUM had the value of 55555, which occupies more than four spaces. In such a case, the space set aside for NSUM will be filled with asterisks, as in ★ ★ ★ ★.

Field descriptors consist of a letter followed by a numeric indication of the number of spaces to be set aside for the variable. The field descriptors used for an output include:

I field—used for integer values.

F field—field used for real values. The usual form is (F total spaces, decimal places). An example is (F9.5), which means a total of nine spaces (including the decimal point) have been set aside for the real variable. The "5" means that five of the nine places will be to the right of the decimal point.

E field—similar in format to the F field, but the value is printed in exponential form.

G field—combines features of both F and E fields. If there is room, the value will be output in F form. If it is too large, output will be in E form

A field—used for character data.

D field—used for double-precision values.

X field—used to insert blank spaces.

L field—used for logical (true or false) values.

H field—used for printing headings and introductory material (such as THE VALUE IS) along with values.

All of these field descriptors may be used for input except the H field. One advantage here is that a READ statement can "slice up" a stream of input data by using a FORMAT statement along with the READ statement. The input data that falls within various fields can then be assigned to various variable names.

Key Punch and Terminal Entry

For many years, FORTRAN programs were entered into a computer by means of a deck of punched cards. Recently, there has been the introduction of video terminals for the entry of FORTRAN programs. There are some differences in the way a FORTRAN program is prepared for entry depending upon whether punched cards or a video terminal is used.

Punched cards are divided into 80 column positions running from left to right across the card. The first column position is used for indicating whether the line is a comment. The first five column positions can be used for line numbers. The sixth column position is reserved for a character indicating the statement is continued from a previous line. Column positions 7 through 72 are used for the FORTRAN statement. The remaining column positions, 73 through 80, are not read by the computer system. They may be left blank; however, they are commonly used to sequentially number the punched cards so as to ensure the statements of the FORTRAN program are in proper order.

The major difference in the format when a video terminal is used is that each line of the program must be assigned a line sequencing number. Line sequencing numbers are normally five digit numbers in the range of 00001 to 99999. The statements will be executed in the order of the values of the line numbers.

Continued statements are indicated by a plus sign (+) in the column position immediately following the line sequencing number. If there is any other character in the column position immediately following the line sequencing number, the line is treated as a comment.

Line sequencing numbers do not replace optional statement numbers. Statement numbers may come between the line sequencing number and the statement itself, as in this example:

```
00010 * THIS IS A COMMENT LINE
00020 100 A = B + C
```

Reserved Words

As a general rule, a keyword should never be used as a variable name. Good programming practice also calls for the practice of not using a keyword as any part of a variable name in order to avoid confusion.

Chapter 7
LISP

LISP is a relatively old language that has recently been the subject of renewed interest due to its suitability for artificial intelligence applications. LISP is an acronym for *LISt* Processing Language. It was developed in 1959 by John McCarthy at the Massachusetts Institute of Technology.

LISP is in many respects totally unlike any other commonly used programming language. It was primarily developed for nonnumeric computation, in direct contrast to other languages. It is also unique in its heavy emphasis upon recursive functions. LISP programs are a list of function definitions followed by the functions to be evaluated. Execution, however, is not in the step-by-step manner of other languages. Each function definition is in the form of an expression. And, as might be expected from the term from which LISP gets its name, there is a heavy emphasis on list structures and notation.

Unfortunately, LISP has been developed in two main versions, EVALQUOTE-LISP and EVAL-LISP, and each system may not have all the functions normally given for its version of LISP. In addition, some functions may have somewhat different meanings on various systems. As such, it is impossible to cover here all the possible variations of LISP. In this chapter, we will restrict our discussion to EVALQUOTE-LISP unless otherwise stated. Also, some functions may have different definitions on some LISP systems than given here. One should always consult the LISP manual for the system being used.

Atoms and Lists

Atoms are the "words" of LISP. They are alphanumeric or numeric quantities such as ZARP, 530, DT43TT9, etc. Some LISP systems require that all atoms begin with a letter. Those are known as *alpha* atoms. Some LISP systems also allow for character strings. These are introduced by the symbols $$ and are "bracketed" by characters not appearing in the character string. For example, the character string CHAR could be bracketed by Y in the form $$YCHARY.

Lists are also "words" as far as the LISP language is concerned. Lists are built up from atoms and other lists. Lists follow the general format:

(any number of atoms and lists)

Some examples of lists are (EXAMPLE OF LIST), (WORD), and (LIST OF 1234). Lists may be joined together to form other lists by the proper placement of parentheses. For example, the "quantities" (THIS IS) and (A LIST) can be joined together to form the list (THIS IS (A LIST)). The placement of parentheses and the order in which lists are read follow the format:

(first list (second list (third list)))

and continue in the same pattern as additional lists are added.

One special list frequently found in LISP is the *null list*. It is simply ( ); it is also written as NIL. Most LISP systems consider NIL to be both an atom and a list. NIL is also used to terminate lists in some LISP systems.

Predicates

The LISP language includes a number of predicate functions that return either T (true) or NIL (false). The ones most commonly found on LISP systems are as follows:

EQ—This has two arguments. Its value is T if both arguments are equal. On most systems, EQ requires both arguments be atoms.
EQUAL—This is the same as EQ but it works with numbers and other arguments. It is "safer" to use this instead of EQ.
NULL—This is true if the value of the argument is NIL.
ATOM—This is true if the argument is an atom.
ZEROP—This is true if the value of the argument is zero.

Program Structure

A LISP program is in reality an extended expression. The expression consists of a function name followed by a list of arguments. Several such extended expressions may follow one another and the LISP will evaluate each one as it comes. The key point to understanding a LISP program is that most functions are defined recursively—they are inherently repetitive. The results of each repetition are usually dependent upon the results of previous repetitions. The ability to write or read a recursively written program is not easily picked up by many persons. Care must be taken to observe the proper placement and matching of pairs of parentheses when reading or writing LISP programs.

Basic Functions

The LISP language has several functions for the manipulation of lists. One is CAR, which gives the *first* element of a list. It is used as in:

CAR (THIS IS A LIST)

which gives THIS.

Another common function is QUOTE. When used with an argument, it gives the argument as a result. For example, the function

QUOTE (THIS IS A QUOTE)

gives THIS IS A QUOTE as a result.

CDR is a function that gives the remaining part of a list after *deleting* the first element of the list. The function:

CDR (THIS IS A LIST)

gives IS A LIST as a result.

CONS is a function that joins short arguments into a single longer one. The function

CONS THIS IS (A LIST)

gives (THIS IS A LIST) as a result.

Some systems also allow for the function LAST. This returns the *last* element of a list. For example,

LAST (THIS IS A LIST)

gives LIST as a result.

APPEND is a function that is available on some systems which *joins* two or more lists. The function

APPEND (THIS IS) (A LIST)

gives the result (THIS IS A LIST).

Some systems have REVERSE available as a function. As the name implies, REVERSE gives the elements of the list in the *opposite* order from which they are in the list. The function

REVERSE (THIS IS A LIST)

gives (LIST A IS THIS) as a result.

User Defined Functions

LISP permits users to define functions without naming them. These functions are known as LAMBDA functions. Their general form is:

(LAMBDA (elements) (expression))

The elements are usually atoms while the expression is an extended list as defined earlier.

Good programming practice calls for naming any new functions defined by the use of the DEFINE function. DEFINE is essentially a variation of the LAMBDA function in the form:

(Function name (LAMBDA (arguments) extended expression))

Once new functions are defined, they are added to the system and may be used like functions supplied in LISP.

PROG

LISP also allows for a more elaborate function known as PROG. PROG is short for "PROGram," and it simplifies the writing of certain types of programs. The PROG function allows for loops, assignment statements, and "go to" types of program control shifts. The evaluation of a PROG statement closely follows the rules by which statements are evaluated in ALGOL. GO TO statements are used with atoms serving as statement labels. The general form of a PROG function is:

(PROG (PROG variables) (arguments))

PROG variables are different alpha atoms. These are local variables used only within the PROG function.

Numeric Functions

While the LISP language is primarily of interest for non-numeric computation, it has functions for numeric computation. Most LISP systems have the following:

ABSVAL—gives the absolute value of an expression.
ADD1—adds one to the value of an expression.
ENTIER—gives the integer part of an expression.
EXPT—one argument is raised to the power of a second argument.
DIFFERENCE—subtracts the following of one argument from another.
FLOAT—gives full decimal representation of an argument.
MAX—gives the largest of a group of arguments.
MIN—gives the smallest of a group of arguments.
PLUS—adds values of arguments together.
QUOTIENT—divides the values of two arguments.
RECIP—gives the reciprocal of an argument.
REMAINDER—gives the remainder after dividing two arguments.
SQRT—gives the square root of an argument.
SUB1—subtracts one from an argument.
TIMES—multiplies arguments together.

Set Functions

LISP also includes several features for the manipulation of sets. The following functions are available on most LISP systems:

INTERSECTION—gives a list of all elements that two sets have in common.

MEMQ—function giving T or NIL if an element is a member of a set.

UNION—gives a list consisting of all elements appearing in two sets.

MAP Functions

Many LISP systems provide for a group of functions known as the MAP functions. They allow writing short programs that perform complex operations. Most MAP functions are used only when all parts of a list are to be considered. The general form of a MAP function is:

```
(MAP function (LAMDA (list value)      ))
```

The MAP function will go through each expression of the list and apply a function to the value of each. The result of a MAP function is a list of values to which the function has been applied. MAP functions go by such names as MAPCAR and MAPLIST, where such functions as CAR and LIST are applied to all elements of a list.

READ and PRINT Functions

The LISP language has READ and PRINT functions. The READ function simply inputs an expression from the input medium. The PRINT function causes an expression to be printed on a new output line. On some systems, the PRINT function will return the value of NIL when used. Some systems also have PRIN1, which causes an expression to be printed out but which does not cause printing on a new line for each expression in the output.

Conditional Expressions

Most versions of LISP allow for conditional expressions through the use of the COND function. The general form of COND is:

```
COND (1 2)
     (3 4)
     (5 6)
```

A COND function is evaluated in the following manner. Argument 1 is evaluated. If it is not NIL, the second argument is evaluated and used as the value of the COND function. If the first argument is NIL, then argument 3 is evaluated. The evaluation of COND proceeds in this manner for all expressions.

Various LISP systems will have features and functions not covered here. Before any attempt is made to interpret a LISP program, it is essential to consult the LISP manual provided for the system that the program was designed to run on.

Chapter 8
Pascal

Pascal is a relatively new language that has achieved wide acceptance in a remarkably short time. It was first put into operation in 1970 by Dr. Niklaus Wirth of Zurich, Switzerland. It was developed from ALGOL and, thus, shares many similarities with that language. Unlike most of the names of computer languages, Pascal is not an acronym; its name is a tribute to the seventeenth century mathematician Blaise Pascal.

Like ALGOL, statements in the Pascal language are separated by semicolons instead of line numbers. It is also block structured like ALGOL—meaning that programs are composed in blocks beginning with BEGIN and terminating with END. Each block is, in effect, an independent program. Pascal programs flow logically from beginning to end without the abrupt shifts back and forth that characterize such languages as BASIC and FORTRAN.

The Pascal language goes beyond ALGOL in allowing the users to define and manipulate new types of data other than the standard integer, real, array, and string types. This is a powerful tool in the hands of a creative programmer.

Program Format

The general format for a Pascal program is:

```
(* comment giving program name or description *)
PROGRAM name (INPUT, OUTPUT);
     Definitions and declarations
BEGIN (* program name *)
. . .
Statements, each of which must end with a semicolon (;)
. . .
END. (*program name*)
     Data
```

Comments may be inserted into the program by placing them inside of the symbols (* . . . *), as shown in the preceding program format. These comments have no effect on the execution of the program and are solely for the convenience and understanding of the programmer and other users. Standard programming practice calls for beginning each program with a comment giving the program name or a description of the program. The program name follows as a comment after BEGIN and END. Comments should also be used to indicate PROCEDUREs, FUNCTIONs, and any potentially confusing blocks of the program.

Each program begins with a heading in the following form:

```
PROGRAM name of program (INPUT, OUTPUT);
```

The program name may be selected from a group of names known as *identifiers*. Identifiers must begin with a letter followed by any combination of letters and digits. Identifiers must not contain operational symbols or spaces, nor can they be words on the Pascal reserved word list. It is also a good programming practice to keep all identifiers distinct from each other in regard to the first eight characters.

Spaces may be used as desired to separate words and symbols in the Pascal language; in fact, separate lines may be used to separate words and symbols. The semicolon (;) must be used to separate individual statements from each other.

The *external files* of the program follow the name of the program in the heading. The external files are contained within parentheses. Normally, each program will have INPUT and OUTPUT as external files. Other files may be established as required. Files other than INPUT and OUTPUT are "automatically" declared whenever used in the heading.

BEGIN and END are used to establish limits for each block of the program. Simple programs may have just one BEGIN/END while more complex programs may have several. The final END in the program is followed by a period (.).

Various types of definitions and declarations follow the heading. Variables are assigned identifiers here and are declared as to type (INTEGER, REAL, etc.). New types of variables that are different from the standard ones provided for in Pascal are established here. Data is input into the program at the end of the program, not in the body of the program.

Variables and Constants

Constants may be declared in Pascal by a CONST statement. An example would be:

```
CONST MILE = 5280
```

Identifiers for constants follow the rules for all identifiers in the Pascal language. CONST statements appear in the definitions and declarations section of the program first, before other statements such as VAR and TYPE.

Every variable that occurs in the Pascal language must be declared by a VAR statement. The VAR statement associates an identifier with each variable and defines its type, as in:

```
VAR MAX, MIN: REAL;
    AMT, RATE: INTEGER;
```

Once declared, a variable's type is permanent. Its actual value may change (as from 10 to 20) but not its type (as from integer to real). Each program block can generally have only one VAR statement. However, as many variables as needed can be declared with a single VAR statement.

The standard variable types in the Pascal language are:

INTEGER—Values that are elements of the set of whole numbers.

REAL—Values that are elements of the set of real numbers.

BOOLEAN—Values that have the logic values of true or false.

CHAR—Values that are strings of letters and digits.

One of the most powerful features of Pascal is the ability for users to define and use value types other than INTEGER, REAL, BOOLEAN, or CHAR. This can be done using a TYPE statement such as the following:

TYPE DAY (SUN, MON, TUES, WED, THUR, FRI, SAT);

Values of the new type will be constants of the new type. The TYPE statements define values of a particular type, not variables of the type. A VAR statement is required to declare variables and must follow the TYPE statements.

Constant definitions and variable declarations may come immediately after the PROGRAM declaration and before any executable statements. When they are located in this manner, they are said to be *global*. Global constants and variables may be used anywhere in the program. In addition, constant definitions and variable declarations may be located within the various blocks of a Pascal program and such definitions and declarations are used within that block; they are known as *local* definitions and declarations. It is possible to use the same identifiers for local definitions and declarations in other blocks, although this is usually poor programming practice.

Assignment Statements

An *assignment statement* computes a value and assigns it to a variable. "Values" are initially assigned to values by inputting data in the order that corresponds to the order in which the variables are declared. Assignment statements can be used to assign new values to variables.

Assignment statements make use of the following operators:

+	Addition with real and integer numbers.
−	Subtraction and negation of real and negative numbers.
*	Multiplication of real and integer numbers.
/	Division with real number result; operands may be real or integer.
DIV	Division giving integer result; both operands must be integers.
MOD	For remainder of integer division.
:=	Generalized equivalence statement; similar to = in conventional algebra.

Assignment statements are executed in the order that they appear in the program from top to bottom and from left to right. Further rules concerning the order of operations are:

1. Expressions in parentheses, regardless of preceding and succeeding operators.
2. Negation.
3. Multiplication and division.
4. Addition and subtraction.
5. Sequences of operations of the same type are done from left to right.

Some examples of assignment statements include:

```
NUM1 := 12
NUM2 := (12*9)/2.57
```

Arrays

An array in Pascal language is a fixed number of data components of the same type that are equally accessible. The ARRAY statement is used to establish an array in the following manner:

ARRAY [index] OF type

The index is generally of the form [1 . .N] with N representing the upper limit of the array. Multidimensional arrays can be declared by using arrays of arrays as follows:

ARRAY [index] OF ARRAY [index] OF type

A type of structure sometimes used with ARRAY statements is PACKED. This reduces the space required in storage by the data structure. PACKED precedes ARRAY, as in:

PACKED ARRAY [index] OF type

PACKED can be used and will have no effect on the meaning of the program, except that PACKED structures cannot be used as actual variable parameters.

ARRAY statements of CHAR type variables use PACKED ARRAY statements. These are used for generating strings in the Pascal language.

Relational Operators

Relationships between expressions are expressed in Pascal through the following operational symbols:

=	Is equal to
<>	Is not equal to
>	Is greater than

> =   Is greater than or equal to
  <   Is less than
< =   Is less than or equal to

Another group of relational operators is used only with BOOLEAN operands. The operators and their meanings are:

AND   Statement is true if both expressions are true.
OR   Statement is true if either expression is true.
NOT   Statement is true if the expression is *not* true.

Control Statements

The Pascal language incorporates several statement classes to control the execution of a program. One group controls the number of times an action is repeated. One of the most common statements is the UNTIL statement:

```
REPEAT
     action
UNTIL
     expression
```

A variation of this is the WHILE statement:

```
WHILE
     expression
DO
     action
```

A more elaborate control statement is the FOR statement. It allows an action to be repeated for an exact number of times. The form of the FOR statement is:

```
FOR variable identifier : = expression TO expression DO
     action
```

Expressions in the FOR statement are usually integers but may be more complex expessions. A variation of the FOR statement substitutes DOWNTO for TO. This allows the statement to move from a higher valued expression to a lower valued expression.

Conditional Statements

Another group of statements selects between the alternatives based upon different conditions. One common statement of this type is the IF/THEN statement. Its form is:

```
IF expression
      THEN statement
```

A variation of IF/THEN adds ELSE as follows:

```
IF expression
    THEN statement
    ELSE statement
```

The GOTO statement is sometimes used in conjunction with other conditional statements. This is the only statement in the Pascal language that makes use of a line number. It is shown as follows:

```
    IF expression THEN GOTO 100
100 expression or statement
```

Line numbers must be declared using a LABEL declaration. LABEL declarations must come before VAR and CONST declarations that follow the PROGRAM heading. The form of a LABEL declaration is:

```
LABEL 100
```

Good programming practice in the Pascal language calls for using the GOTO statement only when no alternative method of structuring the problem exists.

Another useful conditional statement is CASE. It allows the selection among several different alternatives based upon the integer value of an expression. The general form of a CASE statement is:

```
CASE expression OF
    1. statement
    2. statement
    3. statement
       . . .
    N. statement
END (* of CASE statement *)
```

Input and Output Methods

A READ statement is the Pascal statement to input data. Data is inputted in the following manner:

```
READ (NUM1, NUM2, NUM3);
    data
    7 9 14
```

Data comes after the program and the individual data bits are separated by at least one space. Data is assigned to variables in the order in which they are inputted. In the preceding example, NUM1 would have a value of 7, NUM2 would have a value of 9, and NUM3 would have a value of 14.

A READ statement will only input data until it reaches the end of a line. If data is on following lines, the READLN statement must be used. This causes the input control to shift to the next line when the end of the first line containing data is reached. READLN can also be used to only partially read a line of data. For example, if four variables are listed following READLN, only the first four bits of data will be inputted and all succeeding bits on the same line will be ignored.

A WRITE statement is used to output data in Pascal language. Literals can be included in the output by placing them inside of single quotes. If a single quote is needed in the literal, it can be included by using double quotes, which will appear as a single quote in the output. Referring to the data in our READ example, we could have:

```
WRITE ('NUM1' 'S VALUE IS', NUM1);
    NUM1'S VALUE IS 7
```

While similar to READLN, WRITELN causes a shift to another line. Whenever the output specified following WRITELN is output, the program control shifts to the next line. This feature allows creative touches to the output of a Pascal program.

Procedures and Functions

A *function* is a set of actions which may be invoked as needed during program execution; it takes one or more given values and returns a single result. A *procedure* is similar to a function, but can return several results or no results at all. A procedure can "stand alone" as a statement; a function can be used in almost any situation where a constant or variable could be used. In short, procedures can be considered as replacements for statements while functions can be considered replacements for expressions. Both functions and procedures must be declared.

The FUNCTION declaration has the following form:

```
FUNCTION identifier (parameter list) : type;
    BEGIN
        statements
    END;
```

where identifier is a standard Pascal identifier, parameter list represents the parameters used in the function, and type defines the type of the value associated with the function.

Parameters are variables whose values are not assigned to

them by an assignment statement. Instead, values are passed to the parameters from the statement that calls the function or procedure. There is usually another type declaration within the same parentheses as the parameter list which declares the types of the parameters.

Each function or procedure is, in effect, an independent Pascal program. Variables and constants can be declared and defined within a function or procedure just as in the main program. Since each function or procedure is independent of the rest of the program and other functions and procedures, identifiers used in one function or procedure can be repeated again for a different use in another part of the program (although this is not considered good programming practice).

Procedures are declared in a manner similar to functions; with PROCEDURE substituted for FUNCTION. Since a procedure does not itself return a value, there is no type declaration in a PROCEDURE declaration.

Library Functions

ABS—result is the absolute value of X.

ARCTAN—result (REAL) is the arc tangent in radians of X.

CHR—result (CHAR) is a character in the position in the collating sequence given by the argument.

COS—result (REAL) is the cosine of X expressed in radians.

EOF—result is true if the end of file or end of data is reached; otherwise, the result is false.

EOLN—result is true if the end of the line is reached while reading the line; otherwise, the result is reached.

EXP—result (REAL) is **e** raised to power X, where **e** is the logarithmic natural number.

LN—result (REAL) is the natural logarithm of X, X > 0.

ODD—result is true if X is odd; otherwise, it is false. X must be INTEGER.

ORD—result (INTEGER) is the ordinal number of an argument X in the set of values of which X is a member.

PRED—result is the predecessor value relative to the argument value.

RESET—initializes an input file to accept values.

REWRITE—initializes an output file to output data.

ROUND—result (INTEGER) is value of X rounded from a REAL value.

SIN—result (REAL) is sine of X expressed in radians.

SQR—result is square of X.

SQRT—result (REAL) is square root of X.

SUCC—result is successor value relative to the argument value.

TRUNC—result (INTEGER) is value obtained by truncating fractional part of REAL X.

Sets

Pascal allows the mathematical concept of a set to be used in programming. A set may be defined by the definition

SET OF type

where the type must be ordinal. Thus, sets of real numbers or strings are not allowed. Moreover, sets must be processed as a whole since Pascal provides no operations to break a set down into its individual elements.

Pascal includes the following set operators:

*   Intersection
+   Union
−   Difference

Pascal also provides the comparison operator IN. It has the following typical form:

IF variable IN[set] THEN statement

IN can be used in conjunction with other conditional statements and relational operators.

Files

A file is a data structure composed of elements of the same type. Pascal files are sequential; elements may be added, deleted, or examined only by going through the entire file in order. Files may be declared by

identifier: FILE OF type

To generate a file, components are written to it one at a time. The file is readied for writing by the predeclared procedure

REWRITE (file)

which clears the file of all components. To add elements, WRITE is used along with the file identifier and desired component in parentheses. The file identifier and component should be separated by a comma.

A file may be read by using the predeclared procedure RESET followed by the file name in parentheses. This prepares the file reading. The file can then be read by using READ followed by the file name and a variable name in parentheses.

The (INPUT, OUTPUT) declaration following the PROGRAM heading establishes files for input and output. They are known as external files. Additional external files may be added following the PROGRAM heading but they must be declared as a variable in the program. Files used for purposes other than input and output are known as internal files.

Records

A record is a data structure composed of components that may be of different types. It is also a random-access structure and may be updated or modified as desired. The general form of a RECORD declaration is:

TYPE   identifier   RECORD

END   fields

Fields are components of a record.

One problem with records is that their components will be processed by a sequence of statements. It would be much shorter in such cases if separate variables had been declared and used. The WITH statement lets one access the components of a record as if they were simple variables. The general form of a WITH statement is:

```
WITH variables DO
     statements
```

Reserved Word List

AND	END	NIL	SET
ARRAY	FILE	NOT	THEN
BEGIN	FOR	OF	TO
CASE	FUNCTION	OR	TYPE
CONST	GOTO	PACKED	UNTIL
DIV	IF	PROCEDURE	VAR
DO	IN	PROGRAM	WHILE
DOWNTO	LABEL	RECORD	WITH
ELSE	MOD	REPEAT	

Chapter 9
PL/1

PL/1 (Programming Language 1) made its debut in 1965 as an ambitious attempt to combine the best features of FORTRAN, COBOL, and ALGOL into a single language. The result was a language whose capabilities were matched only by its complexity.

The versatility of PL/1 is indeed impressive. Its facilities for scientific calculations rival FORTRAN, and its ability to manipulate nonnumeric data is far superior. Like COBOL, the PL/1 language uses many statements whose meanings are readily self-explanatory, enabling a PL/1 program to be understood with a minimum of trouble by those not familiar with the language. And, some of the more interesting features of ALGOL have been included, although the total capabilities of the PL/1 language are vastly superior to any version of the ALGOL language.

Shortly after the introduction of the PL/1 language, it was predicted by many that PL/1 would be the single most important programming language of the 1970s. However, PL/1 fell far short of matching the FORTRAN and COBOL languages in popularity and, by the end of the decade, was slipping behind such languages as Pascal and BASIC in total usage. Part of the reason for the failure of PL/1 to meet the expectations planned for it is the complexity of the language; most implementations of the PL/1 language include over 200 keywords. Only a small portion of the capabilities of PL/1 can be utilized in most programming applications—the language is simply "too big" for many purposes. Also, the PL/1 language was introduced after the FORTRAN and COBOL languages were firmly entrenched. Many COBOL and FORTRAN users had no pressing need for the additional facilities of PL/1 and did not switch to the new language.

PL/1 still remains an interesting and impressive language. The sheer size of the language prevents us from covering all of its features in this chapter; only the most common and useful features will be mentioned. More complete information should be obtained from a system manual or user report.

Program Format

Any PL/1 program—either the main program or a subroutine—is called a *procedure* and must begin with the word PROCEDURE. All procedures must have a label preceding them. The PROCEDURE statement for the main program takes the form of:

label: PROCEDURE OPTIONS (MAIN);

and terminates with the word END. Likewise, all subroutines have a label before PROCEDURE and terminate with END. Labels may consist of up to 31 characters, and the first character must be a letter of the alphabet. All labels must be separated from statements by a colon (:). Sometimes a "break" symbol __ will be used in labels, as in TIME__OF__DAY.

Semicolons (;) are used to separate the statements from each other. Two or more statements may be placed on the same line (although normal programming practice discourages this). Each statement *must* end with a semicolon.

Comments may be inserted into a program by placing them between the symbols/ * and */, such as:

/* comments */

Comments may be inserted between statements or even between the separate terms of a statement.

Program execution normally flows from top to bottom, although this can be modified through the use of the various control transfer statements and labels.

All PL/1 keywords and variable names must be separated from each other by at least one blank space. However, there must be no blank spaces within variable names. The break symbol __ should be used when necessary to improve readability of variable names.

Variables and the DECLARE Statement

Variable names in the PL/1 language may consist of up to 31 characters, the first of which must be a letter of the alphabet. The symbols $, @, and # may be included as part of a variable name.

Numbers are stored in various forms by the PL/1 compiler. One form is REAL FIXED BINARY. In this form of internal representation, the number 8 would be stored as 1000.B, with 1000 being the base 2 equivalent of the decimal 8, followed by a decimal point and the letter B to denote the quantity is binary. Similarly, a number such as .125 would be stored as .001B.

Another form of storage is REAL FLOAT DECIMAL. This form uses a mantissa, then the letter E and a number referring to a base of ten. Some examples of REAL FLOAT DECIMAL numbers are 6.2E2, 5.E0, -87.1E6, and 3.3E-5.

Variables beginning with the letters I through N are automatically stored as REAL FIXED BINARY, while variables beginning with the other letters of the alphabet are stored as REAL FLOAT DECIMAL. This assignment can be overridden by the DECLARE statement.

A DECLARE statement allows specifying the *attributes* of variables. For example, the variable name LATITUDE would normally have its value represented in the computer in REAL FIXED BINARY form. But it can be stored in REAL FLOAT DECIMAL form by using the following format:

DECLARE LATITUDE REAL FLOAT DECIMAL;

Another common form of internal representation is REAL FLOAT BINARY, which is similar to REAL FLOAT DECIMAL except that the number is "exponential binary." A typical form is 1101E2B, with the B again indicating binary.

Some versions of PL/1 also allow for a COMPLEX attribute which allows for internal representations of complex numbers. However, the CHARACTER attribute is more common. This allows the variable name to represent a string of up to 256 alphanumeric characters. It is established by the following typical statement:

DECLARE NAME CHARACTER (15);

which allows NAME to be the name of a character string of 15 characters. The attribute VARYING indicates that the length of the string varies. For example,

DECLARE NAME CHARACTER (15) VARYING;

indicates that NAME is the name of a string that can contain up to 15 characters.

Closely related to the CHARACTER attribute is the BIT declaration. This declares a variable name that is used to represent strings of the specified number of binary digits.

A variable name can be used to represent any label used in the program by using the attribute LABEL with DECLARE. It is used in the following manner:

DECLARE A12345 LABEL;

which establishes a label named A12345. Labels are used with loops.

The STOP Statement

The STOP statement causes program execution to cease. Program execution normally ceases when the END statement is encountered; STOP can be used to terminate execution of the program in other areas of the program (as a consequence of an IF . . . THEN statement, for example).

Operational Symbols

The PL/1 language uses the following operational symbols:

+	Addition
–	Subtraction
*	Multiplication
/	Division
**	Exponentiation
=	Equals
¬ =	Not equal
<	Less than
< =	Less or equal to
>	Greater than
> =	Greater or equal to
&	AND
|	OR
¬	NOT
||	Concatenation

The normal sequence of operation is for exponentiation to be performed first, followed by multiplication and division. Next comes addition and subtraction, then concatenation, relational operations and, finally, AND/OR operations. The ¬ symbol can be used to negate any relational expression. Operations are normally performed from left to right, with the exception of operations contained in parentheses which are always performed first. The concatenation symbol is only used with operations involving strings, whether bit or character.

The INITIAL Specification

When used with a DECLARE statement, INITIAL allows the setting (initializing) of the values of variables. For example, the statement

DECLARE SUM FIXED INITIAL (500);

would cause the value 500 to be stored in SUM in REAL FIXED DECIMAL form.

Arrays

An array may be set up using a DECLARE statement. The general form used is:

DECLARE variable name (lower limit: upper limit) attributes;

Thus, the statement DECLARE SUM (1:10) would set up an array of SUM1, SUM2, etc., through SUM10. Additional dimensions can be specified by separating the index ranges by a comma, as in:

DECLARE SUM (1:10, 1:5) REAL FLOAT DECIMAL;

which will set up an array of SUM having index ranges for its two dimensions of 1 through 10 and 1 through 5. Index ranges can be declared in terms of arithmetic expressions which are evaluated to define the index ranges.

Names of arrays may be included in arithmetic operations without indices. In such cases, the arithmetic operation will be performed for each value for the index range. Sometimes, the first index value will be omitted when establishing a variable. In such cases, the lower index value will be assumed to be 1.

Sometimes the asterisk (*) will be used to denote the entire range of an index. Suppose an array has been established for SUM with the ranges 1 to 5 and 1 to 3. Thus, SUM (2, *) will denote the array SUM(1,1), SUM(1,2), and SUM (1,3). This is sometimes referred to as *cross-sectioning* an array.

Control Statements

The PL/1 language includes several statements used to alter normal execution flow of a program. One of the simplest, GO TO, transfers execution to a labeled portion of the program. Its form is simply:

    GO TO statement label;

and causes control to automatically shift to the point indicated.

A conditional statement is the IF/THEN statement. Its form is:

    IF condition THEN consequence;

which will cause the execution of the consequence depending on whether or not the condition is met. An alternative form is the IF/THEN/ELSE statement:

IF condition THEN first consequence ELSE second consequence;

which will cause the execution of the first consequence if the condition is met or the execution of the second consequence if the condition is not met.

Loops can be set up through the use of DO/END statements, as in:

    DO;
    Statements
    END;

This will cause the loop to be executed once. Multiple executions can be set up by adding TO:

    DO beginning index TO ending index;
    Statements
    END;

which will cause the loop to be performed once for each index value. Normally, the index count will advance by 1 each time the loop is performed. If a different advance is wanted, BY can be added after the ending index and the desired advance specified after BY. There is no requirement in the PL/1 language for the beginning and ending index values or advance increments to be positive integers.

A WHILE notation can be used to cause the execution of a loop as long as a condition is met. The general form is:

```
DO beginning index TO ending index BY increment WHILE
    condition;
Statements
END;
```

An alternative form of conditional loop execution involves a variation of the IF/THEN loop. This is shown by the form:

```
IF condition THEN DO;
Statements
END;
```

An IF/THEN/ELSE statement can also be modified for use with loops in the following manner:

```
IF condition THEN DO;
First set of statements
END;
ELSE DO;
Second set of statements;
END;
```

Procedures

As mentioned earlier, PL/1 programs are made up of procedures. The main program itself is called the *main* procedure and begins with a program name followed by PROCEDURE OPTIONS (MAIN) as mentioned before. Other procedures may be included in the PL/1 program as needed. Procedures are identified by a name and they follow the form:

```
name: PROCEDURE;
Statements
END;
```

When a procedure is to be used, the statement:

```
CALL procedure name;
```

is used. When END is found in the procedure, it returns to the main program of the statement immediately following CALL. A RETURN statement within the procedure itself (for example, as a consequence of a conditional statement) will cause the same result.

If procedures in a program are arranged so that all the executable statements are located between PROCEDURE and END, the procedures are *external* to each other. Variable names and DECLARE statements are used only within each procedure. However, certain parameters (variable names, values, etc.) may be "transmitted" to and from a procedure by placing them in parentheses following the CALL statement.

A *BEGIN block* is similar to a procedure. It follows the form:

```
BEGIN;
Statements
END;
```

A BEGIN block is not executed by a CALL statement but, instead, is executed in the normal sequence of the program. However, all DECLARE statements in a BEGIN block are used only within the block, much like a procedure.

Recursive Procedures

PL/1 allows "recursive" functions (that is, functions that use themselves in their own definition). To define a recursive procedure, the keyword RECURSIVE must appear before the RETURN keyword. The usual form is:

```
name PROCEDURE (argument) RECURSIVE;
    statements;
    RETURN (argument);
```

The PICTURE Specification

A PICTURE specification is used to describe a character string. Each position within the string can be restricted to a single type of character, such as a letter of the alphabet, a numeral, a blank, etc. The following characters are used to make up a PICTURE specification:

X	Any character
A	A through Z, or a blank
B	Blank
V	Position of a suppressed decimal point
V.	. (period or decimal point)
.V	. (period) or blank if preceding character was replaced by a blank
Z	Replaces leading zeroes with blanks
S	Indicates + or −
9	0 through 9
,	, (comma) or blank if preceding character was replaced by a blank
+	+ character (positive)
−	− character (negative)
$	$ character

For example, the PICTURE 'AAAA' specifies a character string such as NAME or HOME. The specification '99999' is for a string of numeric characters such as 27514 and 92514. A PICTURE such as 'XXXXX' could be used for any combination of five characters. Note that all PICTURE specifications are enclosed in single quotes.

PICTURE specifications are established using a DECLARE statement:

DECLARE SUM PICTURE 'XXXXXXXX';

The PICTURE specification means that numerical quantities can be stored and manipulated as character strings.

Library Functions

PL/1 includes the following library functions as part of the language:

ABS—Returns the absolute value of an argument.

ACOS—Returns the arc cosine in radians.

ASIN—Returns the arc sine in radians.

ATAN—Returns the arc tangent in radians.

ATAND—Returns the arc tangent in degrees.

CEIL—Returns the smallest integer greater than or equal to the argument specified.

COS—Returns the cosine in radians.

COSD—Returns the cosine in degrees.

EXP—Returns the natural number e raised to a specified power.

FLOOR—Returns largest integer not greater than the argument.

LOG—Returns natural logarithm of argument specified.

MAX—Finds largest value of two or more arguments.

MIN—Finds smallest value of two or more arguments.

MOD—Returns the remainder of an integer division.

ROUND—Rounds a given value at a specified digit.

SIGN—Returns a 1 if the sign of an argument is positive, a −1 if the sign of the argument is negative, and a 0 if the argument is zero.

SIN—Returns the sine of an argument in radians.

SIND—Returns the sine of an argument in degrees.

SQRT—Returns the square root of an argument.

TAN—Returns the tangent of an argument in radians.

TAND—Returns the tangent of an argument in degrees.

TRUNC—Drops the fractional part of an argument and replaces it with zero.

Other library functions are often supplied by PL/1 systems; consult the system manual for information on those available on a given system.

String Manipulation Statements

The PL/1 language has several features for handling character strings. One of the most commonly used is the concatenation operator, ||. This symbol puts together two character strings into a single new one. Suppose A is the string NEW and B is the string STRING. The statement

    C = A || B

would result in C representing the string NEWSTRING.

PL/1 has several built-in functions for string operations. One is LENGTH. The LENGTH function gives a REAL FIXED BINARY value equal to the number of characters in a string. Its general form is:

    variable name = LENGTH (name of string);

Another function is INDEX. The INDEX function examines two character strings to see if one string is a substring (is part of) of another string. If one string is not a substring of another, the INDEX function gives it a value of 0. If it is a substring, the INDEX function gives it a REAL FIXED BINARY value equal to the position in bytes where one string first appears as a substring of the other. The general form is:

    INDEX (first string, second string);

The INDEX function tests to see if the second string is a substring of the first.

A SUBSTR function will produce a substring of a string. It has the general form:

SUBSTR (string name, beginning position, length);

The beginning position is an integer representing the number of characters from the beginning of the string that the substring starts. The length is an integer representing how many charac-ters of the string the substring will cover from the beginning position. If the length is omitted, the substring will have all the characters from the beginning position to the end of the string.

The TRANSLATE function can replace characters in strings with other characters. Its general form is:

TRANSLATE (string 1, string 2, string 3);

Every time the first character of string 3 occurs in string 1, it is replaced by the first character in string 2. In the same way, each time the second character of string 3 occurs in string 1, it is re-placed by the second character in string 2. This process con-tinues for each character and occurrence. String 2 and string 3 must be of the same length.

Two other string functions are STRING and VERIFY. The STRING function combines elements of an array into a single character string, while the VERIFY function searches one character string for characters not in a second string.

Input and Output Statements

There are two general forms of input and output statements in the PL/1 language. If the data must be converted from one form into binary, it is termed *stream-oriented*; if the data is in binary form only, it is said to be *record-oriented*.

One very common stream-oriented input statement is GET EDIT. It causes data to be read and assigned to variable names according to specified parameters. The general form is:

GET EDIT (variables) (parameters);

Data may be output in a similar fashion by the PUT EDIT statement, which follows the same general format as the GET EDIT statement.

The parameters used for GET EDIT and PUT EDIT statements are as follows:

F(n)	Fixed point numbers, with n representing the total number of characters.
F(n, d)	Same as F(n), except that d represents the number of places to the right of the decimal point.
E(n)	Floating point numbers, with n representing the total number of characters.
E(n, d)	Same as E(n), except that d represents the number of places to the right of the decimal point.
A(n)	Character strings, with n representing the total number of characters.
B(n)	Bit strings, with n representing the length in bits.
X(n)	Results in n number of characters to be skipped on input, or n number of blanks to be inserted on output.

The GET LIST statement reads in a list of variable names separated by commas. If the variables are part of an array, the entire array will be read in if the subscripts are not indicated. The PUT LIST statement causes data items to be printed in a readable form without the use of format parameters.

Closely related to the preceding statements are GET DATA and PUT DATA statements. Variable names may be used in both statements, although array names can be used only in PUT DATA statements. Suppose that the input is A = 10. It can be input into the computer using the statement GET DATA(A). On the output, the statement PUT DATA(A) would result in the output:

A = 10

A READ statement is used for the input of record-oriented data with a WRITE statement being used for the output of the same type of data. Most commonly, they are used with input and output files, which are set up by a DECLARE statement and a FILE specification. A typical declaration would be

DECLARE DISK1 FILE RECORD INPUT

which would establish DISK1 as a record-oriented data file used only for input to memory. An output file could be established just as easily by substituting OUTPUT for INPUT in the DE-CLARE statement. Files may be used for both input and output by using OPEN and CLOSE statements. Once a file has been declared to be INPUT and OUTPUT, OPEN and CLOSE statements can "reset" the file so that it can be used for the opposite function.

The PL/1 language allows a wide variety of data structures and files, much like the COBOL language. However, due to their complexity (and the difficulty in duplicating them in other languages), we will not discuss them here. A PL/1 system manual or user report should be consulted for more detailed information.

Reserved Words

There are no reserved words in the PL/1 language. Good programming practice calls for not using any keyword as the names of variables, files, etc.

Appendix
Keyword Dictionary

The language that each keyword is extracted from is given after each definition.

ABS—Library function giving the absolute value of X (*BASIC*).

ABS—Gives absolute value of an expression (*FORTH*).

ABS—Library function giving the absolute value of a real number (*FORTRAN*).

ABS—Library function giving the absolute value of X (*Pascal*).

ABSVAL—Function giving the absolute value of an argument (*LISP*).

ACCEPT—Used in conjunction with FROM to input small quantities of data (*COBOL*).

ACCESS—Clause specifying MODE by which records are accessed in a file (*COBOL*).

ACOS—Library function giving the arc cosine of X (*FORTRAN*).

ADD—Verb adding two or more data items (*COBOL*).

ADD1—Function adding one to the value of an argument (*LISP*).

AINT—Library function truncating a real value to lowest whole number *(FORTRAN)*.

ALOG—Library function giving the natural logarithm of X *(FORTRAN)*.

ALOG10—Library function giving the common logarithm of X *(FORTRAN)*.

ALTER—Verb used to change the point in a program where GO TO shifts control to *(COBOL)*.

AMAX0—Library function giving the largest of two or more integer values, result is given in real form *(FORTRAN)*.

AMAX1—Library function giving largest of two or more real values *(FORTRAN)*.

AMIN0—Library function giving the minimum of two or more integer values, result is given in real form *(FORTRAN)*.

AMIN1—Library function giving the smallest of two or more real values *(FORTRAN)*.

AMOD—Library function giving the remainder for a real number division *(FORTRAN)*.

AND—Logical operator indicating an expression is true if both expressions in the expression are true *(BASIC)*.

AND—Logical operator combining two elements into an expression that is true if both elements are true *(COBOL)*.

AND—Performs a logical AND operation *(FORTH)*.

AND—Boolean operator indicating that an expression is true if both elements are true *(Pascal)*.

APPEND—Function returning a list composed of all the objects in two lists *(LISP)*.

ARCTAN—Library function giving the arc tangent in radians of X *(Pascal)*.

ARRAY—Declaration establishing an array of variables of a certain type *(ALGOL)*.

ARRAY (OF)—Definition specifying a structure consisting of a fixed number of components *(Pascal)*.

ASC—String function giving the decimal ASCII value of a designated string variable *(BASIC)*.

ASIN—Library function giving the arc sine of X *(FOR-TRAN)*.

ASSIGN (TO)—Statement that is used to assign an integer constant representing a statement number to a simple integer variable *(FORTRAN)*.

ATAN—Library function giving the arc tangent of X *(FORTRAN)*.

ATAN2—Library function giving the arc tangent of Y divided by X *(FORTRAN)*.

ATN—Library function giving the arc tangent of X *(BASIC)*.

ATOM—Function returning T if argument is an atom or NIL if it is not *(LISP)*.

ATOMLENGTH—Function returning a value equal to the number of atoms in a list *(LISP)*.

AUTHOR—Paragraph in identification division giving name of programmer(s) *(COBOL)*.

AUTO—Command starting automatic line numbering at a certain number and increasing by a fixed increment *(BASIC)*.

BACKSPACE—Statement moving a tape or disk back to the beginning of the previous file *(FORTRAN)*.

BEEP—Produces a "beep" sound from the speaker *(BASIC, IBM implementation)*.

BEGIN—Statement starting a sequence of statements *(ALGOL)*.

BEGIN—Used in conjunction with END to denote the limits of a compound statement or an entire program *(Pascal)*.

BEGIN—Statement beginning a series of statements that are executed together in normal program sequence; it does not need a CALL statement to be executed nor does it need a label *(PL/1)*.

BEGIN . . . UNTIL—Performs an operation until the condition following UNTIL is true *(FORTH)*.

BINARY—Attribute indicating a variable is stored in exponential form using a base 2 number system *(PL/1)*.

BIT—Attribute indicating a variable is a bit string of a length equal to a specified number of binary digits *(PL/1)*.

BLOCK CONTAINS—Clause giving size of a specified file description *(COBOL)*.

BLOCK DATA—Heading for a subprogram containing only declaration statements *(FORTRAN)*.

BOOLEAN—Declaration denoting a variable having the values "true" and "false" *(ALGOL)*.

BOOLEAN—Type of variable whose value is either "true" or "false" *(Pascal)*.

BREAK—Statement causing an immediate exit from a SWITCH statement *(C)*.

BY—Indicates increments by which the index of a DO loop is increased *(PL/1)*.

CALL—Statement causing BASIC language program to branch to a machine language subroutine *(BASIC)*.

CALL—Verb used in conjunction with USING causing program control to program the portion that is named *(COBOL)*.

CALL—Statement causing execution of a subroutine depending upon the evaluation of arguments following the name of the subroutine *(FORTRAN)*.

CALL—Statement causing the execution of the procedure that is named *(PL/1)*.

CAR—Function giving the first element of a list *(LISP)*.

CASE—Precedes alternatives in a SWITCH statement *(C)*.

CASE—Used in conjunction with OF to indicate alternatives according to different values of an expression *(Pascal)*.

CDR—Function returning an argument less the first element *(LISP)*.

CHAIN—Transfers control to another program in the "chain" *(BASIC, IBM implementation)*.

CHAR—Defines a single byte character data type *(C)*.

CHAR—Type of variable that is a set of characters *(Pascal)*.

CHARACTER—Statement declaring a variable to be a character variable *(FORTRAN)*.

CHARACTER—Attribute indicating the name of a string of characters *(PL/1)*.

CHR—Library function giving a result that is a character in the position in the collating sequence given by the argument *(Pascal)*.

CHR$—String function that gives a single element string which has an ASCII code that is given by an expression. The value of the expression must be in the range of 0 to 255 *(BASIC)*.

CIRCLE—Draws a circle on the screen *(BASIC, IBM and Apple implementations)*.

CLEAR—Command setting all program variables to zero *(BASIC)*.

CLOAD—Command loading a program from a cassette *(BASIC)*.

CLOSE—Verb ending file processing *(COBOL)*.

CLOSE—Statement which specifies that a file is not set to input or output data *(PL/1)*.

CMOVE—Copies bytes from one memory location to another *(FORTH)*.

CODE—Statement specifying a literal that identifies print lines as being part of a specific report *(COBOL)*.

COLOR—Selects color of video display *(BASIC, IBM and Apple implementations)*.

COMMENT—Declaration that the material that follows is a nonexecuted remark *(ALGOL)*.

COMMON—Passes variables to programs in a chain of programs *(BASIC, IBM implementation)*.

COMMON—Statement specifying that a group of variables is to be kept in an area of common storage *(FORTRAN)*.

COMPLEX—Statement declaring a variable to have a complex value *(FORTRAN)*.

COMPLEX—Attribute indicating a variable is a complex number *(PL/1)*.

COMPUTATIONAL—Clause identifying a type of data USAGE for data items used in computations. They must be numeric and pictures for them can contain only 9, S, V, P, or parentheses *(COBOL)*.

COMPUTE—Verb evaluating an arithmetic expression and assigning it to a data item *(COBOL)*.

CON—Same as CONT in some versions of BASIC *(BASIC)*.

CONS—Function returning a single list from two separate lists *(LISP)*.

CONST—Declaration used to give names to quantities that do not change throughout a program *(Pascal)*.

CONSTANT—Defines a two byte constant name *(FORTH)*.

CONT—Command continuing program execution after a STOP or END statement *(BASIC)*.

CONTINUE—Terminates a loop *(C)*.

CONTINUE—Statement used to terminate a DO loop *(FORTRAN)*.

CONTROL—Clause creating levels of a control hierarchy for a report *(COBOL)*.

COPY—Verb inserting a library text into a program during compilation *(COBOL)*.

CORRESPONDING—Phrase used with ADD, SUBTRACT, or MOVE to allow corresponding data items from two groups to be used as operands in arithmetic without specifying them *(COBOL)*.

COS—Library function giving the cosine of X in radians *(BASIC)*.

COS—Library function giving the cosine of X *(FORTRAN)*.

COS—Library function giving the cosine of X in radians *(Pascal)*.

COSH—Library function giving the hyperbolic cosine of X *(FORTRAN)*.

CSAVE—Command causing program to be saved on a cassette *(BASIC)*.

CURSOR—Statement locating cursor at horizontal point X and vertical point Y *(BASIC)*.

DATA—Used in conjunction with READ to specify data to be input *(BASIC)*.

DATA—Statement used to assign values to variables *(FORTRAN)*.

DATA RECORD—Clause used in a file description to declare names of data records in the file *(COBOL)*.

DECIMAL—Attribute indicating a variable is a number with a decimal point *(PL/1)*.

DECLARE—Statement specifying the attributes of a variable *(PL/1)*.

DEF FN—Defines a user-defined function *(BASIC)*.

DEFAULT—Label used for a case which is executed if none of the other cases in a SWITCH construct is executed *(C)*.

DEFINE—Function returning a list of user-defined functions that have been added to the LISP system *(LISP)*.

DEFINED—Attribute indicating a character string is a portion of a larger one or that an array is part of a higher dimension array *(PL/1)*.

DEL—Same as DELETE in some versions of BASIC *(BASIC)*.

DELETE—Command deleting lines in a program *(BASIC)*.

DELETE—Verb removing a record *(COBOL)*.

DEPTH—Counts numbers on the stack *(FORTH)*.

DIFFERENCE—Function giving the difference in value between two arguments *(LISP)*.

DIM—Command causing space to be allocated in memory for array variables *(BASIC)*.

DIMENSION—Statement setting up an array of variables *(FORTRAN)*.

DISPLAY—Statement used to output literals and other low-volume data *(COBOL)*.

DIV—Operator for division of nonnegative integer values, resulting in truncated integer results *(Pascal)*.

DIVIDE—Verb dividing one data item into another *(COBOL)*.

DO—Statement causing an action to be performed *(ALGOL)*.

DO—Used in conjunction with various statements (WHILE, FOR, CASE, etc.) to cause the execution of an action *(Pascal)*.

DO—Statement indicating the start of a sequence of statements which are to be executed in loop fashion *(PL/1)*.

DO . . . LOOP—Establishes a loop of repetitively performed statements *(FORTH)*.

DOUBLE—Defines a double-precision floating point data type *(C)*.

DOUBLE PRECISION—Statement declaring a variable to be a double-precision type *(FORTRAN)*.

DOWNTO—Used in conjunction with FOR to indicate the range over which an operation is performed, starting from a value and decreasing down the range *(Pascal)*.

DRAW—Draws a line or shape on the video display *(BASIC, IBM and Apple implementations)*.

DROP—Discards top number on the stack *(FORTH)*.

DSP—Statement causing the printing of a variable and the line number where it is executed *(BASIC)*.

DUP—Duplicates top number on the stack *(FORTH)*.

DYNAMIC—Used with ACCESS to indicate a MODE where a file must have indexed organization *(COBOL)*.

EDIT—Command allowing editing of a specific program line *(BASIC)*.

ELSE—Used in conjunction with IF/THEN statements to indicate an alternative to a condition not being met *(ALGOL)*.

ELSE—Used in conjunction with IF to cause execution of a statement when a certain condition is not met *(BASIC)*.

ELSE—Specifies an alternative action to an IF statement *(C)*.

ELSE—Used in conjunction with IF and THEN to indicate a second alternative to a condition *(FORTRAN)*.

ELSE—Used in conjunction with IF to cause the execution of a statement when a certain condition is not met *(Pascal)*.

ELSE—Statement used to create alternative action if a condition is not met *(PL/1)*.

END—Statement ending a sequence of statements *(ALGOL)*.

END—Statement stopping program execution *(BASIC)*.

END—Statement denoting the end of a program *(FORTRAN)*.

END—Used in conjunction with BEGIN to denote the limits of a compound statement or an entire program *(Pascal)*.

END—Statement used to terminate a program or loop *(PL/1)*.

ENDFILE—Statement indicating that the end of a data file has been reached *(FORTRAN)*.

ENTER—Verb allowing more than one language to be used in a COBOL program *(COBOL)*.

ENTIER—Function giving the integer part of an argument *(LISP)*.

ENTRY—Reserved keyword not currently implemented (reserved for future use) *(C)*.

EQ—Function returning T if both atoms are identical or NIL if they are not *(LISP)*.

EQUAL—Function returning T if both elements are identical or NIL if they are not *(LISP)*.

EQUIVALENCE—Statement allowing two or more names to be used for the same variable *(FORTRAN)*.

EXAMINE—Verb counting or replacing a character within a data item *(COBOL)*.

EXECUTE—Statement used to cause the execution of a remote programming block *(FORTRAN)*.

EXIT—Verb providing an ending for a program or a group of procedures *(COBOL)*.

EXP—Library function giving value of natural number *e* raised to a specified power *(BASIC)*.

EXP—Library function giving the natural number *e* raised to a specified power *(FORTRAN)*.

EXPT—Function causing one argument to be raised to the power of a second argument *(LISP)*.

EXTERN—Declares an external variable *(C)*.

EXTERNAL—Statement declaring subprogram names to be used as arguments when calling other subprograms *(FORTRAN)*.

FILE (OF)—Definition used with TYPE to set up a data structure of components of the same type *(Pascal)*.

FILL—Fills designated number of consecutive bytes with byte indicated *(FORTH)*.

FILLER—Elementary item of a record that cannot be directly referenced *(COBOL)*.

FIXED—Attribute indicating a variable is written without exponential notation *(PL/1)*.

FLASH—Causes video display to alternate foreground and background colors *(BASIC, Apple implementation)*.

FLOAT—Declares a floating point data type *(C)*.

FLOAT—Library function giving the real form of an integer value *(FORTRAN)*.

FLOAT—Function giving the floating point form of an argument *(LISP)*.

FLOAT—Attribute indicating a variable is in exponential form *(PL/1)*.

FOR—Statement used to indicate beginning point of a repeated action *(ALGOL)*.

FOR—Statement used in conjunction with NEXT to create loop *(BASIC)*.

FOR—Establishes a repetitively executed loop *(C)*.

FOR—Used in conjunction with TO or DO to control the number of times a sequence of operations is performed *(Pascal)*.

FORMAT—Statement used in conjunction with an input or output statement to specify field descriptors *(FORTRAN)*.

FROM—Used to denote the variable, array, or structure that data is transferred out of *(PL/1)*.

FUNCTION—Statement assigning a name to a subroutine and establishing its arguments *(FORTRAN)*.

FUNCTION—Declaration used to identify a set of actions used to compute a pointer or scalar value *(Pascal)*.

GENERATE—Verb causing a report to be produced according to specifications in the report section *(COBOL)*.

GET—Statement used for the input of stream data *(PL/1)*.

GET EDIT—Statement causing data to be input and assigned to variables or rearranged internally *(PL/1)*.

GET STRING . . . EDIT—Statement used to select items from a single character string *(PL/1)*.

GOSUB—Statement causing program to branch to subroutine at specified line number *(BASIC)*.

GO TO—Statement causing program control to shift to point indicated by a label *(ALGOL)*.

GO TO—Verb shifting program control to another part of the program *(COBOL)*.

GO TO—Statement transferring control to another line number *(FORTRAN)*.

GO TO—Unconditional statement transferring program to a labeled statement *(PL/1)*.

GOTO—Statement causing control to shift to a specific line number *(BASIC)*.

GOTO—Transfers control to a labeled statement *(C)*.

GOTO—Used with a statement label to shift the program control to another statement in the program *(Pascal)*.

GR—Sets video display to low resolution mode *(BASIC, Apple implementation)*.

HCOLOR—Sets video display color in high resolution graphics mode *(BASIC, Apple implementation)*.

HLIN—Draws a horizontal line *(BASIC, Apple implementation)*.

HOME—Returns cursor to upper left of screen *(BASIC, Apple implementation)*.

IABS—Library function giving the absolute value of an integer *(FORTRAN)*.

IF—Expression used in conjunction with THEN and sometimes ELSE to make execution of statements dependent upon a condition being met *(ALGOL, BASIC)*.

IF—Precedes condition in a conditional construct *(C)*.

IF—Verb used with THEN and ELSE to indicate a condition and its consequences *(COBOL)*.

IF—Statement causing another statement to be executed depending upon a condition *(FORTRAN)*.

IF—Used in conjunction with THEN or ELSE to make execution of a statement conditional upon a certain condition *(Pascal)*.

IF—Statement used with THEN to perform some action if a condition is met (PL/1).

IF . . . THEN—Performs action following THEN if top of stack is true (FORTH).

IMPLICIT—Statement declaring all variables beginning with the same letter to be of the same type (FORTRAN).

IN—Operator used to indicate whether a value is a member of a set (Pascal).

INARRAY—Primitive procedure causing an array of real values to be input (ALGOL).

INDEX—Statement indicating that a data item is an index type (COBOL).

INDEX—Function of two character strings giving a FIXED BINARY value of 0 if the second string is not a substring of the first; otherwise, the value is the position in bytes where the second string begins to appear as a substring of the first string (PL/1).

ININTEGER—Primitive procedure causing integer values to be input (ALGOL).

INITIAL—Used with DECLARE to set the values of variables (PL/1).

INP—Reads a byte from a port specified by an integer expression in the range 0 through 255 (BASIC).

INPUT—Enters data into memory and assigns it to variables following INPUT (BASIC).

INPUT—Verb causing data to be entered into a COBOL program (COBOL).

INPUT—Attribute specifying that a file is to be used only for input into memory (PL/1).

INREAL—Primitive procedure causing a real value to be input (ALGOL).

INSPECT—Verb counting or replacing a character within a data item (COBOL).

INSYMBOL—Primitive procedure causing alphanumeric data to be input (ALGOL).

INT—Library function giving integer portion of an expression that is less than or equal to the expression (BASIC).

INT—Declares an integer data type *(C)*.

INT—Library function converting a real value to an integer value *(FORTRAN)*.

INTARRAY—Primitive procedure causing an array of integer values to be input *(ALGOL)*.

INTEGER—Declaration denoting a variable contains only integer values *(ALGOL)*.

INTEGER—Statement declaring a variable to be an integer *(FORTRAN)*. ·

INTEGER—Variable type whose values are all whole numbers *(Pascal)*.

INTERSECTION—Function giving the intersection of the objects in two sets *(LISP)*.

INITIATE—Verb causing the start of report processing *(COBOL)*.

INTO—Used to denote the variable, array, or structure that data is input to *(PL/1)*.

ISIGN—Library function transferring the sign of one integer value to another *(FORTRAN)*.

JUSTIFIED—Clause that gives the positioning of data within a data item *(COBOL)*.

LABEL—Assigns a statement label number to a statement *(Pascal)*.

LABEL—Variable type with a label as a value *(PL/1)*.

LABEL RECORD—Clause indicating whether there are any label records in a file description *(COBOL)*.

LAMBDA—Construction doing away with the requirement for defining new function names *(LISP)*.

LAST—Function returning the last element of a list *(LISP)*.

LEADING—Description of the leftmost character in a string *(COBOL)*.

LEFT$—Function allowing movement of characters from the left end of a string into another string *(BASIC)*.

LEN—Function returning the full length of a string *(BASIC)*.

LENGTH—Function giving the number of elements in the first line of a list *(LISP)*.

LENGTH—Function giving a FIXED BINARY value equal to the number of characters in a character string *(PL/1)*.

LET—Statement assigning a value to a variable *(BASIC)*.

LINE-COUNTER—Special register for each report description found in the report section of data division *(COBOL)*.

LINE INPUT—Statement allowing printing of a prompting message and inputting of a string *(BASIC)*.

LIST—Command causing the listing of the lines in a program *(BASIC)*.

LIST—Function giving a list of the values of a group of arguments *(LISP)*.

LOCK—Verb ending file processing *(COBOL)*.

LONG—Declares long integer data type *(C)*.

MAP—Function that applies the value of a function to all elements of a list *(LISP)*.

MAX—Leaves greater of two numbers *(FORTH)*.

MAX—Function returning the largest value of a group of arguments *(LISP)*.

MAX0—Library function giving the largest of two or more integer values *(FORTRAN)*.

MAX1—Library function giving the largest of two or more real values, with the result converted to integer form *(FORTRAN)*.

MEMSET—Function returning T if an object is a member of a particular set *(LISP)*.

MERGE—Verb combining two or more files *(COBOL)*.

MID$—Function allowing movement of characters from the middle of one string to another *(BASIC)*.

MIN—Leaves lesser of two numbers *(FORTH)*.

MIN—Function giving the smallest value of a group of arguments *(LISP)*.

MINUS—Function giving the negative value of an argument *(LISP)*.

MIN0—Library function giving the smallest of two or more integer values *(FORTRAN)*.

MIN1—Library function giving the smallest of two or more real values with the result converted to integer form *(FORTRAN)*.

MOD—Operator giving the remainder of a division *(BASIC)*.

MOD—Leaves remainder from a division *(FORTH)*.

MOD—Library function giving the remainder of an integer division *(FORTRAN)*.

MOD—Operator giving the remainder for division of integer values *(Pascal)*.

MOTOR—Controls cassette motor *(BASIC, IBM implementation)*.

MOVE—Verb transferring data to other data items *(COBOL)*.

MOVE—Copies numbers from one memory location to another *(FORTH)*.

MULTIPLY—Verb multiplying two data items *(COBOL)*.

NAMELIST—Statement allowing input and output of several variables without a FORMAT statement by calling one name *(FORTRAN)*.

NEGATE—Leaves two's complement *(FORTH)*.

NEW—Deletes current program and clears all variables *(BASIC)*.

NEXT—Used in conjunction with FOR to create loop *(BASIC)*.

NIL—The empty list; also frequently used to end a list *(LISP)*.

NOT—Logical operator negating a statement or operand *(COBOL)*.

NOT—Reverses value of status flag *(FORTH)*.

NOT—Boolean operator indicating the expression is true if one element of the expression is not true *(Pascal)*.

NOTE—Verb indicating that the material, which follows, is a comment *(COBOL)*.

NOTRACE—Same as TROFF in some versions of BASIC *(BASIC)*.

OCCURS—Clause indicating subscripts of data items *(COBOL)*.

OF—Used in conjunction with CASE to indicate alternatives according to different values of an expression *(Pascal)*.

ON—Used in conjunction with GOSUB and GOTO to cause program to move to a specific line *(BASIC)*.

ON ENDFILE—Statement specifying instructions to be executed when an "end of file" mark is found by a READ statement *(PL/1)*.

OPEN—Verb making files available for processing *(COBOL)*.

OPEN—Statement which specifies a file is set to input or output data *(PL/1)*.

OR—Logical operator indicating statement is true if either expression is true *(BASIC)*.

OR—Performs logical OR operation *(FORTH)*.

OR—Function returning a T if either argument is T, or NIL if both arguments are NIL *(LISP)*.

OR—Boolean operator indicating the expression is true if either element of the expression is true *(Pascal)*.

ORGANIZATION—Clause indicating whether a file is organized in sequential, relative, or indexed form *(COBOL)*.

OUT—Statement causing byte specified by a second expression to be sent to port specified by the first expression, values of both expressions must be in range 0 through 255 *(BASIC)*.

OUTARRAY—Primitive procedure causing an array of real values to be output *(ALGOL)*.

OUTINTEGER—Primitive procedure causing an integer to be output *(ALGOL)*.

OUTPUT—Attribute specifying that a file is to be used only for output of data from memory *(PL/1)*.

OUTREAL—Primitive procedure causing the value of a real variable to be output in floating-point form *(ALGOL)*.

OUTSTRING—Primitive procedure causing literals to be output *(ALGOL)*.

OUTSYMBOL—Primitive procedure causing alphanumeric data to be output *(ALGOL)*.

OUTARRAY—Primitive procedure causing an array of integer values to be output *(ALGOL)*.

OVER—Copies second number on top of the stack *(FORTH)*.

PACKED ARRAY—Similar to ARRAY, but instructs the compiler that storage should be economized, at the cost of inefficiency in being accessed *(Pascal)*.

PACKED RECORD—Similar to RECORD, but instructs the compiler that storage should be economized at the cost of some inefficiency when being accessed *(Pascal)*.

PAGE—Clause that defines length of a page and its vertical subdivisions *(COBOL)*.

PAINT—Paints a designated area of the screen a selected color *(BASIC, IBM implementation)*.

PAUSE—Statement causing program execution to temporarily pause and a message to be printed *(FORTRAN)*.

PEEK—Function reading the value of a memory location specified by an expression *(BASIC)*.

PERFORM—Verb transferring program control to specified paragraph *(COBOL)*.

PICK—Copies designated number to the top of the stack *(FORTH)*.

PICTURE—Clause describing a data item *(COBOL)*.

PICTURE—Specification used to describe a character string in which character is restricted to an indicated type *(PL/1)*.

PLAY—Plays specified music *(BASIC, IBM implementation)*.

PLUS—Function adding together the values of a group of arguments *(LISP)*.

POKE—Statement causing byte specified by a second expression to be stored in a location specified by the first expression *(BASIC)*.

POS—Gives a number indicating current cursor position on video display *(BASIC)*.

PRINT—Statement outputting data specified by a variable or literal *(BASIC)*.

PRINT—Statement causing a variable or literal to be output *(FORTRAN)*.

PRINT—Function causing an element to be sent to an output device *(LISP)*.

PRINT @—Statement causing printing at a specified position *(BASIC)*.

PRINT USING—Statement specifying PRINT format *(BASIC)*.

PROCEDURE—Statement assigning a name to a group of statements *(ALGOL)*.

PROCEDURE—Declaration defining part of a program and giving it an identifier that is used to call it *(Pascal)*.

PROCEDURE—Follows name of and identifies subprograms or subroutines of main program *(PL/1)*.

PROCEDURE OPTIONS (MAIN)—First line in program; follows program name *(PL/1)*.

PROCEED—Verb changing point in a program where GO TO shifts control *(COBOL)*.

PROG—Function consisting of a list of variables followed by a list of arguments *(LISP)*.

PROGRAM—Heading denoting the beginning of a program, including program name and the parameters by which the program communicates with its environment *(Pascal)*.

PUT—Statement used for output of stream data *(PL/1)*.

PUT EDIT—Statement causing data to be either output through an output device or rearranged internally *(PL/1)*.

PUT STRING ... EDIT—Statement used to combine several items into a single string *(PL/1)*.

QUOTE—Constant with a value of one or more quotation characters *(COBOL)*.

QUOTE—Function returning the exact value of an argument *(LISP)*.

QUOTIENT—Function dividing one argument by another *(LISP)*.

RANDOM—Used with ACCESS to indicate a MODE where a file must have indexed organization *(COBOL)*.

READ—Statement assigning values in DATA statement to numbers or string variables *(BASIC)*.

READ—Verb moving a record from a file and making it available for processing *(COBOL)*.

READ—Statement causing data to be input *(FORTRAN)*.

READ—Function causing an element to be read into a system from an input device *(LISP)*.

READ—Statement used to input data to assign values to variables *(Pascal)*.

READ—Statement used to transfer record-oriented data from external memory into the computer *(PL/1)*.

READLN—Statement which reads data in a manner similar to READ but which causes a skip to the next line of data *(Pascal)*.

REAL—Declaration denoting a variable contains real number values *(ALGOL)*.

REAL—Statement declaring a variable to be a real value *(FORTRAN)*.

REAL—Type of variables whose values are real numbers. This type of variable can generally accept whole numbers as well *(Pascal)*.

REAL—Attribute indicating a variable is a real number *(PL/1)*.

RECIP—Function giving the reciprocal of an argument *(LISP)*.

RECORD—Structure type consisting of a fixed number of components that may be of different types *(Pascal)*.

RECORD CONTAINS—Clause in the file description specifying size of data records *(COBOL)*.

RECURSIVE—Identifies procedure that is recursive; i.e., it can call itself *(PL/1)*.

REDEFINES—Clause allowing a second data name to define a storage area *(COBOL)*.

REGISTER—Places variables in processor registers *(C)*.

RELEASE—Verb transferring records to the first sequence of SORT action *(COBOL)*.

RENAMES—Clause giving alternative groupings of elementary items *(COBOL)*.

REPEAT—Used in conjunction with UNTIL to indicate that an action is to be repeated until the expression following UNTIL is true *(Pascal)*.

REM—Nonexecutable statement for program clarity and user convenience *(BASIC)*.

REMARKS—Clause indicating a comment follows *(COBOL)*.

REN—Same as RENUM in some versions of BASIC *(BASIC)*.

RENUM—Command renumbering lines in a program to allow insertion of new lines *(BASIC)*.

REPORT—Clause used to name reports in the report file *(COBOL)*.

REPORT SECTION—Part of data division that contains report descriptions *(COBOL)*.

RERUN—Clause specifying when and where rerun information is recorded *(COBOL)*.

RESERVE—Clause specifying the number of input/output areas allocated to a file *(COBOL)*.

RESET—Standard procedure allowing file scanning *(Pascal)*.

RESTORE—Statement allowing data in DATA statements to be re-read *(BASIC)*.

RESUME—Command causing program execution to resume at a specific line *(BASIC)*.

RETURN—Statement causing program to branch to statement following last GOSUB *(BASIC)*.

RETURN—Returns a function to its caller *(C)*.

RETURN—Verb getting records from last phase of MERGE and SORT actions *(COBOL)*.

RETURN—Statement transferring execution from a subroutine to the main program *(FORTRAN)*.

RETURN—Statement in a procedure causing a return to the calling program *(PL/1)*.

RETURNS—Statement specifying the attributes for the form of a value produced by a procedure *(PL/1)*.

REVERSE—Function causing the objects in a list to be reversed *(LISP)*.

REWRITE—Discards sequence currently associated with a file and allows it to receive a new sequence *(Pascal)*.

RIGHT$—Function allowing movement of characters from the right end of a string into another string *(BASIC)*.

RND—Function returning a random number between 0 and 1 *(BASIC)*.

ROLL—Rotates designated number to top of the stack *(FORTH)*.

ROT—Rotates third number to top of the stack *(FORTH)*.

ROUNDED—Clause causing a result to be rounded to the nearest least-significant digit *(COBOL)*.

RUN—Command starting execution of a program. If a line number is given, execution starts at specified line *(BASIC)*.

RUN—Follows STOP to end program execution *(COBOL)*.

SAME—Clause causing two or more files to share the same area during processing *(COBOL)*.

SCRATCH—Deletes current program and clears all variables. Used instead of NEW in some systems *(BASIC)*.

SEARCH—Verb that scans a table for a data item meeting specified conditions *(COBOL)*.

SECURITY—Paragraph in identification division that can be followed by a comment *(COBOL)*.

SEGMENT-LINE—Clause varying the number of permanent segments in a program *(COBOL)*.

SELECT—Clause associating a file with an external file; used in conjunction with ASSIGN *(COBOL)*.

SET—Statement assigning values to index data items *(COBOL)*.

SET (OF)—Definition establishing a set of objects of the same type *(Pascal)*.

SETQ—Function with an alpha atom and an argument which gives the alpha atom the value of the argument *(LISP)*.

SGN—Function returning the sign (positive or negative) of an expression *(BASIC)*.

SHORT—Defines a short integer data type *(C)*.

SIGN—Library function transferring the sign of one real value to another *(FORTRAN)*.

SIN—Library function giving the sine of an expression *(BASIC)*.

SIN—Library function giving the sine of a real value *(FORTRAN)*.

SINH—Library function giving the hyperbolic sine of a real value *(FORTRAN)*.

SIZEOF—Operator which computes the size of an object *(C)*.

SKIP—Statement causing the input or output to skip to the next record *(PL/1)*.

SORT—Verb creating a sort file that sorts records and makes them available in sorted order *(COBOL)*.

SOURCE—Clause used in a report to identify data item moved to a printable item *(COBOL)*.

SOURCE-COMPUTER—Paragraph in the environment division describing computer on which program is compiled *(COBOL)*.

SPACE—Constant representing the space character *(COBOL)*.

SPACE$—Function giving a string of spaces whose length is specified by the expression which follows *(BASIC)*.

SQR—Library function giving square root of an expression *(BASIC)*.

SQRT—Library function giving the square root of X *(FORTRAN)*.

SQRT—Function giving the absolute value of an argument *(LISP)*.

STATIC—Defines a permanent, "private" variable type *(C)*.

STEP—Statement indicating how the beginning value of a repeated action is increased *(ALGOL)*.

STEP—Used with FOR/NEXT loop to indicate increments in which loop travels over a range of values *(BASIC)*.

STOP—Statement stopping program execution *(BASIC)*.

STOP—Verb used with literal to temporarily end execution of a program *(COBOL)*.

STOP—Statement causing the execution of a program to stop *(FORTRAN)*.

STRING—Function combining elements of an array or structure into a single string *(PL/1)*.

STR$—Function giving a string representation of an expression *(BASIC)*.

STRUCT—Defines a structure array *(C)*.

SUBROUTINE—Statement assigning a name to a self-contained program *(FORTRAN)*.

SUBSTR—Function defining a substring of a string along with its number of characters and the letter of the string where substring begins *(PL/1)*.

SUB1—Function subtracting one from the value of an argument *(LISP)*.

SUBTRACT—Verb subtracting one data item from another *(COBOL)*.

SUM—Clause setting up a sum counter in a report group description and designating data items summed into the counter *(COBOL)*.

SWAP—Statement causing the value of two variables to be exchanged *(BASIC)*.

SWAP—Exchanges top two numbers on a stack *(FORTH)*.

SWITCH—Declaration causing program control to shift to labeled points depending upon the value of an index variable *(ALGOL)*.

SWITCH—Sets up a set of alternative cases *(C)*.

SYNCHRONIZED—Clause specifying how elementary data items are stored *(COBOL)*.

SYSTEM—Statement allowing loading of machine language programs and data *(BASIC)*.

TAB—Function causing spacing to horizontal position indicated *(BASIC)*.

TALLY—Special register used in conjunction with EXAMINE *(COBOL)*.

TAN—Function giving the tangent of an expression in radians *(BASIC)*.

TAN—Library function giving the tangent of X *(FORTRAN)*.

TANH—Library function giving the hyperbolic tangent of X *(FORTRAN)*.

TERMINATE—Verb causing report processing to be completed *(COBOL)*.

THEN—Used in conjunction with IF to indicate consequence of a condition *(ALGOL)*.

THEN—Used in conjunction with IF to cause execution of a statement when specified condition is met *(BASIC)*.

THEN—Used in conjunction with IF to indicate a consequence for a condition *(FORTRAN)*.

THEN—Used in conjunction with IF to cause the execution of a statement when a condition is met *(Pascal)*.

THEN—Used in conjunction with IF for a conditionally executed action *(PL/1)*.

TIMES—Function multiplying several arguments *(LISP)*.

TO—Used in conjunction with FOR to indicate the range over which an operation is performed *(Pascal)*.

TO—Indicates ending index for a DO loop *(PL/1)*.

TRACE—Same as TRON in some versions of BASIC *(BASIC)*.

TRACE—Function showing the different arguments another function takes and their values *(LISP)*.

TRANSLATE—Function that replaces individual characters in a string with other characters *(PL/1)*.

TROFF—Statement turning off trace function activated by TRON *(BASIC)*.

TRON—Activates trace function giving line number of each line as it is executed to illustrate program flow *(BASIC)*.

TYPE—Clause in the report group description specifying the particular type of report group *(COBOL)*.

TYPE—Statement used on some systems in place of PRINT *(FORTRAN)*.

TYPE—Declaration allowing definition of value types other than real, integer, or Boolean *(Pascal)*.

TYPEDEF—Defines identifiers which can be used like type keywords *(C)*.

UNION—Function resulting in the union of the objects of two sets *(LISP)*.

UNTIL—Statement indicating the ending point of a repeated action *(ALGOL)*.

UNTIL—Used in conjunction with REPEAT to indicate an action is repeated until the expression following UNTIL is true *(Pascal)*.

UNTRACE—Function whose argument is a list of function names that will no longer be TRACEd *(LISP)*.

UPDATE—Attribute specifying that a file can be used for both input and output from memory *(PL/1)*.

USAGE—Clause specifying manner in which a data item is represented in storage *(COBOL)*.

USR—Function allowing calling of machine language subroutine *(BASIC)*.

VAL—Function returning numerical value of a string *(BASIC)*.

VALUE—Declaration that a parameter is to be transferred by value instead of name *(ALGOL)*.

VALUE IS—Clause defining value of constants *(COBOL)*.

VALUE OF—Clause giving a certain value to a data item in the label record of a file *(COBOL)*.

VAR—Declaration giving a list of identifiers denoting new variables and their types *(Pascal)*.

VARIABLE—Creates a two byte variable name *(FORTH)*.

VARPTR—Function giving memory address of a variable and its value *(BASIC)*.

VARYING—Attribute indicating the length of a character string will change during program execution *(PL/1)*.

VERIFY—Function that searches a string for a character not in a second string *(PL/1)*.

VLINE—Draws a vertical line *(BASIC, Apple implementation)*.

VTAB—Moves cursor to line specified *(BASIC, Apple implementation)*.

WAIT—Statement of first port is joined with second port by AND and joined with third port by XOR, causing program to stop and await a nonzero result *(BASIC)*.

WHILE—Statement indicating an action is to be performed so long as a certain condition is being met *(ALGOL)*.

WHILE—Statement causing execution of a loop or another statement as long as a condition is met *(FORTRAN)*.

WHILE—Used in conjunction with DO to perform an action as long as a controlling statement is true *(Pascal)*.

WHILE—Statement indicating a loop is performed as long as a condition is met *(PL/1)*.

WHILE. . .WEND—Sets up a loop which is executed as long as a condition is true (*BASIC*, IBM implementation).

WIDTH—Command setting the width in characters of a printing terminal line (*BASIC*).

WITH—Statement enabling access to the components of a record as though they were simple variables (*Pascal*).

WRITE—Verb producing printout of a record (*COBOL*).

WRITE—Statement causing output in specified field descriptors (*FORTRAN*).

WRITE—Statement causing expressions to be output together (*Pascal*).

WRITE—Statement used to transfer record-oriented data from the computer to external memory (*PL/1*).

WRITELN—Statement causing expressions to be output on a single line (*Pascal*).

XOR—Logical operator causing statement to be true if both elements are different from each other (*BASIC*).

XOR—Performs a logical exclusive-OR operation (*FORTH*).

ZERO—Constant representing the value or character 0 (*COBOL*).

ZEROP—Function resulting in T if argument is zero, NIL if value is not zero (*LISP*).

Computer Language Books!

C PRIMER PLUS
Gives you a clear, complete introduction to the C programming language, its usage and programming methods. By Waite, Prata, and Martin. 448 pages, 7½ x 9½, softbound. ISBN 0-672-22090-3. © 1984.
Ask for No. 22090 . . . . **$17.95**

BASIC PROGRAMMING PRIMER (2nd Edition)
Gives you fundamental keywords, statements, and functions usable with the IBM PC, Apple®II, or any other computer running a variation of Microsoft BASIC. By Waite and Pardee. 384 pages, 6 x 9, comb-bound. ISBN 0-672-22014-8. © 1982.
Ask for No. 22014 . . . . **$17.95**

BASIC: FUNDAMENTAL CONCEPTS
Introduces and compares DEC and Microsoft BASIC, teaches you how to convert programs from one BASIC dialect to another, and more. By Joseph C. Giarratano. 198 pages, 8½ x 11, softbound. ISBN 0-672-21941-7. © 1982.
Ask for No. 21941 . . . . **$22.95**

BASIC: ADVANCED CONCEPTS
Helps you explore the limitations of floating-point arithmetic, examine number systems commonly used in computing, and more. By Joseph C. Giarratano. 214 pages, 8½ x 11, soft. ISBN 0-672-21942-5. © 1982.
Ask for No. 21942 . . . . **$22.95**

COBOL ON MICROCOMPUTERS
Guides experienced computerists in using two powerful compilers for CIS COBOL and LEVEL II COBOL on a microcomputer, and points out the extra features of these two versions compared to standard ANS COBOL. By Alan D. T. Fryer 144 pages, 5½ x 8½, softbound. ISBN 0-672-22230-2. © 1984.
Ask for No. 22230 . . . . **$8.95**

FORTH PROGRAMMING
Shows you the differences between FORTH-79 and fig-FORTH, how to write or modify programs in either dialect, and more. By Leo J. Scanlon. 246 pages, 5½ x 8½, softbound. ISBN 0-672-22007-5. © 1982.
Ask for No. 22007 . . . . **$16.95**

INTRODUCTION TO FORTH
Covers general FORTH programming plus particulars of MMS FORTH. Many programming examples provided and compared to the Level II BASIC version of the same program for clarity. By Ken Knecht. 142 pages, 5½ x 8½, softbound. ISBN 0-672-21842-9. © 1982.
Ask for No. 21842 . . . . **$10.95**

PASCAL PRIMER
Guides you through UCSD™ Pascal program structure, procedures, variables, decision-making statements, and numeric functions. By Waite and Fox. 208 pages, 8½ x 11, comb-bound. ISBN 0-672-21793-7. © 1981.
No. 21793 . . . . **$17.95**

PASCAL WITH YOUR BASIC MICRO

Teaches you Pascal and includes a pseudo-Pascal compiler usable with Microsoft BASIC, Applesoft, or BBC. By Jeremy Rushton. 136 pages, 5½ x 8½, softbound. ISBN 0-672-22036-9. © 1983.
Ask for No. 22036 . . . .**$9.95**

APPLE® FORTRAN

Gives you full programming details on Apple FORTRAN 77, plus several programs in FORTRAN that you can use immediately, and more. By Blackwood and Blackwood. 240 pages, 6 x 9, comb-bound. ISBN 0-672-21911-5. © 1982.
Ask for No. 21911 . . . .**$14.95**

APPLESOFT LANGUAGE (2nd Edition)

Quickly introduces you to Applesoft syntax and programming, including advanced programming techniques, graphics, color commands, sorts, searches, and more. By Blackwood and Blackwood. 288 pages , 6 x 9, comb-bound. ISBN 0-672-22073-3. © 1983.
Ask for No. 22073 . . . .**$13.95**

ATARI® BASIC TUTORIAL

Leads you through the practical ins and outs of ATARI BASIC programming, including color graphics and sound. By Robert A. Peck. 224 pages, 6 x 9, comb-bound. ISBN 0-672-22066-0. © 1983.
Ask for No. 22066 . . . .**$12.95**

BASIC PROGRAMMING WITH THE IBM PCJR®

Contains a detailed BASIC tutorial, plus programming hints and many useful sample programs you can enter and run. By David C. Willen. 286 pages, 8 x 9¼, softbound. ISBN 0-672-22359-7. © 1984.
No. 22359 . . . .**$12.95**

TIMEX SINCLAIR BASIC PRIMER WITH GRAPHICS

Thanks to T/S 1000 graphics, you "see" your commands work as your own programs gradually develop into runnable realities. By Waite and Chapnick. 160 pages, 8 x 9¼, softbound. ISBN 0-672-22077-6. © 1984.
Ask for No. 22077 . . . .**$9.95**

These and other Sams Books and Software products are available from better retailers worldwide, or directly from Sams. Call 800-428-SAMS or 317-298-5566 to order, or to get the name of a Sams retailer near you. Ask for your free Sams Books and Software Catalog!

Prices good in USA only. Prices and page counts subject to change without notice.